Taking Up Space

7/19

Please return/renew this item by the last
date shown. Books may also be renewed
by phone or internet.

www3.rbwm.gov.uk/libraries

01628 796969 (library hours)

0303 123 0035 (24 hours)

# TAKING UP SPACE

## *The Black Girl's Manifesto for Change*

Chelsea Kwakye and Ọrẹ Ogunbiyi

1 3 5 7 9 10 8 6 4 2

#Merky Books
20 Vauxhall Bridge Road
London SW1V 2SA

#Merky Books is part of the Penguin Random House group of companies
whose addresses can be found at global.penguinrandomhouse.com.

Penguin
Random House
UK

First published by #Merky Books in 2019

www.penguin.co.uk

A CIP catalogue record for this book is available from the British Library.

ISBN 9781529118537

Printed and bound in Great Britain by Clays Ltd, Elcograf S.p.A.

Penguin Random House is committed to a sustainable future
for our business, our readers and our planet. This book is made from
Forest Stewardship Council® certified paper.

MIX
Paper from
responsible sources
FSC® C018179
FSC
www.fsc.org

# Contents

### Adaobi.

Adaobi Adibe is an Electrical and Electronic Engineering (BEng) student at the University of Manchester. She was the lead Venture Capitalist at Campus Capital, a £2.5 million fund investing in early stage technology companies. Her work in Venture Capital and clean energy led to her being awarded the number one black student in the UK by the prestigious Future Leaders magazine, and nominated by the U.S. embassy as one of the top six rising entrepreneurs in the UK.

### Arenike.

Arenike Adebajo is a content producer working across the arts and publishing industries. She graduated from the University of Cambridge with a First Class degree in English. At university, she served as the facilitator for

FLY, a forum for women and non-binary people of colour and co-edited the group's first zine.

### Ayomide.

Ayomide Ayorinde is a 4th year medical student at Imperial College London, currently intercalating a BSc in Management into her degree. She currently works for the Imperial College Outreach Team. Outside of this, she was director of the 2017/18 Afrogala, Imperial College ACS's annual cultural show, and before this, the Vice-President of the society.

### Barbara.

Barbara Falana is currently studying Medicine at King's College London. She has interests in social mobility and innovation technology. She has worked and continues to work closely with the student access and social mobility team within her university. She is currently working as the beneficiary director for Step Forward, a social enterprise with the intention of preventing soil-transmitted diseases such as Mossy Foot which is heavily prevalent in underdeveloped countries.

## Courtney.

Courtney Daniella Boateng is a Human, Social and Political Sciences graduate from the University of Cambridge. She found a love for honest and relatable content creation as well as public speaking leading to her speaking at multiple universities and press features in Teen Vogue, Buzzfeed, BBC and many others. Transitioning from being a full time hairstylist simply to sustain herself and her family, she found herself pursuing entrepreneurship and began consulting on business development for other beauty brands focussing on Black Hair & Beauty whilst also consulting for 10 Downing Street and the National Union of Students (NUS) on how best to aid young entrepreneurs and financially support students in poverty.

## Eireann.

Eireann Attridge is an Education and English graduate from the University of Cambridge. Growing up in a single parent working class household in South London, she became concerned with factors that influenced educational disadvantage. She later went on to serve as the Student Unions' Access and Funding Officer, running the country's largest student led access initiative and also established the Cambridge Class Act campaign, a campaign for students who identify as being from working class and educationally disadvantaged backgrounds. After university, Eireann worked in a school in East London, supporting students to apply to university and designing programmes around university preparedness. Currently, she is studying for an MSc in Education (Higher Education) at the University of Oxford and has an offer to start her PhD there in 2019. Eireann aims to work within university administration and admissions in order to make universities an inclusive space.

### Fope.

Fope Olaleye is a student at the University of Newcastle where they study Politics. During their time at university they were elected BAME Network President, Feminist Society President and NUSU Part Time Officer. They also sat on the NUS Black Students Committee and National Executive Council as Black Students Campaign second place, and they are now the NUS Black Students' Officer. In these roles Fope has campaigned to improve the experiences of BAME students across the UK with a particular focus on black women and QTIPOC. They have been featured in *Dazed*, *i-D* and on BBC Radio 1xtra, and are a regular guest speaker and workshop facilitator at universities across the country.

### Kenya.

Kenya Greenidge is a Human, Social and Political Sciences graduate from the University of Cambridge. While she was there she served as Cambridge ACS's Secretary 2016/17 and played an active role in the society's executive committee. She has a particular interest in the sociology of race and gender.

### Micha.

Micha Frazer-Carroll is an award-nominated journalist writing on race, feminism and mental health. Formerly working at HuffPost UK, Micha is the arts and culture editor at gal-dem, a magazine created by women and non-binary people of colour, and founded Blueprint, a magazine on mental health. With bylines in *ROOKIE*, *Black Ballad* and *Dazed*, she now writes regularly for the *Guardian*. After graduating with first class honours in Psychology and Sociology, Micha served as Cambridge University's Welfare and Rights Officer in 2017-18, a role in which she lobbied the University Counselling Service to introduce a counselling scheme catered specifically to students of colour.

## Mikai.

Mikai McDermott is a digital content creator and entrepreneur offering 'life advice, beauty and the tablespoon of honesty you need.' Her growing cult following has earned her over 2 million YouTube views, over 30k subscribers and over 30k followers on Instagram. A bold and proud advocate for women's issues, fashion and beauty, the University of Warwick graduate has crafted a niche for herself as a trusted opinion among the underground beauty community. Having collaborated with BBC Stories, Tangle Teezer and Schwarzkopf (among others), Mikai has worked on authentic collaborations with high engagement rates anchored by informative content. Alongside building an online presence, Mikai runs a hair and beauty brand which has amassed more than 10k followers in just under a year.

## Nathania.

Nathania Williams is studying history at the University of Cambridge. She is of Jamaican heritage but most of her family now live in Manchester, which is where she's from. She is passionate about access to higher education and mental health issues in the black community. She was Cambridge ACS's Welfare Officer and now serves as the society's Vice President. She is currently active in her college's Feminist Society and FLY, a forum for women and non-binary people of colour, as well as a member of Trinity College's History Society.

## Renée.

Renée Kapuku is currently a postgraduate student at Harvard Graduate School of Education. During her time as an undergraduate at the University of Oxford, she was elected as the first BME representative at her Oxford college, and worked with the Oxford Campaign for Racial Equality to tackle racial discrimination on campus. Renée was also elected president of the Oxford African and Caribbean society in her second year, hosting Oxford's first black history month showcase with Reggie Yates, and organising the #BlackMenAndWomenOfOxford viral campaign. She coordinated the UK's largest student-led conference for high-achieving Year 12 state-school students of African and Caribbean heritage, receiving critical acclaim from the BBC, general media, and support from the elected Person of the Year, Stormzy. Earlier this year, Renée was awarded full funding by the Kennedy Memorial Trust to support her studies in International Education Policy at Harvard.

## Saredo.

Saredo Qassim Mohamed is a Somali-Canadian writer and photographer. She is currently pursuing a Master's degree at the London School of Economics and Political Science in the International Migration and Public Policy Programme. During her undergraduate years, she became a Canadian National Youth Poetry champion and represented the city of Toronto in international poetry festivals. As the President of Western University's Black Students' Association, Saredo worked to create spaces of healing and community for black students on her campus. After graduating, she worked with a local NGO in Somalia to promote the social and political empowerment of vulnerable Somali women and girls.

## Saskia.

Saskia Ross is currently a student at the London Academy of Music and Dramatic Arts. They graduated from the University of Cambridge with a degree in Human, Social and Political Sciences. While at university, Saskia primarily worked in theatrical spaces and laid the groundwork for a more diverse and welcoming scene, becoming dedicated to widening participation in a historically elite and white community. They created the Cambridge BME Group, an online space where students of colour could share ideas, promote their work and find a safe community of like-minded people. They then directed Cambridge's inaugural BME Shakespeare performance, and one of Cambridge's largest all-black casts in a production of Fences by August Wilson. They also facilitated the creation of BME Footlights smokers and musical theatre bar nights.

## A Letter to My Fresher Self

In December 2017, inspired by her own experiences and those of her peers and mentees, Ọrẹ wrote a letter to her fresher self about what it means to be a black girl at Cambridge. The letter was published in her student newspaper, *Varsity*, and read as follows:

> **When you walk into your first supervision, you will probably be the only black girl in the room. Get used to it, because it won't get much better. But don't let that scare you and, more importantly, don't let anyone make you feel small or misplaced. Don't be silent in attempts to assuage your white**

peers and supervisors. You've earned your place there, so make your presence known. Don't ever feel the need to make yourself palatable, or bite-size. Instead, fill the room with examples of Nkrumah and Mobutu that your supervisor thinks are 'adventurous', and enjoy unpacking the racism in the works of Kant that your degree so glorifies. *Their* discomfort is not your problem.

You will have supervisors who will call you defensive and angry, and who will project their own prejudiced stereotypes onto you as you walk into the room. Cry in private, write a killer essay, and prove them wrong. You will also have supervisors who will understand and appreciate your need to veil your work in your own experiences, who will recognise its value and reward you for it. So, bathe every essay in black girl magic and write in resistance to the Eurocentrism of academia that did not see you coming.

It's not always easy, though. The Black Jacobins you really want to read probably won't be on your reading lists, you won't find the support you need when you want to write your dissertation on Nigeria, and trying to go the extra mile to show your supervisors what a decolonised curriculum *could* look like will exhaust you. But where you can, do it anyway.

Don't be surprised when your lecture on industrialisation makes no mention of slavery, or
when your white friends don't understand why
that's a problem. Don't be afraid to ask the
unnerving questions at the end of the lecture
and leave them shook.

You will arrive and feel a pressure to be someone
else. You won't realise as you subconsciously try
to play up to what you think a typical Cambridge
student does. You'll change your accent, go to
events you know you don't enjoy, and try to
befriend people that aren't like you in attempts
to conform – but you'll only be able to keep this
up for so long. When the real you resurfaces and
you find the courage to admit to your new
friends, and to yourself, that you actually hate
Wednesday Cindies [a terrible Cambridge student club night] and VKs, you'll be okay.

When you come back next term with braids, don't
let your housemates smell and touch your hair. It
may take you a while to muster up the courage to
tell people to stop, and to remind people that you
are not some exotic creature to be caressed – but
when you find the strength, do it anyway.

Oh. Boys? Don't bother. Tell every aunty that is
telling you that you are going to Cambridge to

find yourself a husband, that much to their disappointment, it's not going to happen. You'll learn quickly that desirability is racialised and that not everyone loves your dark skin as much as you do, that society's beauty standards don't include people that look like you. So, when someone hits you with 'you're fit for a black girl', tell them that's not a compliment. You are beautiful, and to the people who don't see that, even your own, let it be their loss. Find the beauty in your blackness in spite of the people who can't.

Don't forget that, regardless, you belong here. You'll have people who think you are here to tick a 'diversity' box. You will also be asked time and time again whether or not you go to the *other* university in Cambridge because people will have a tough time conceptualising the fact that you could possibly have earned your place here. You won't find people who look like you memorialised on the walls and that won't make it any easier – but don't forget that you belong.

You will stand out and be made conscious of your difference for your whole time here and not everyone will get it. Not everyone will get what it is about existing in Cambridge as a black girl that makes it difficult or why. You will meet a lot of people who proclaim they are 'not racist' but don't recognise how their inaction makes them complicit, why you value safe spaces, or even why your experience of Cambridge is necessarily different. Remember that it isn't your duty to lecture and to explain because the emotional labour will take its toll. You are not the appointed spokesperson for black people, and don't feel the pressure to be.

Remember that you are not alone. Black women may be few and far between here, but find them, build a sisterhood and strengthen each other. Find shoulders to cry on because you will need them. Find support systems that work for you, and take solace in them. Communities like the African Caribbean Society will be there to make you feel at home again. Take time to look after yourself. Bake and cook jollof even amid the stress that tries to break you.

It will get better. I don't know if that's because you will become immune to the blows, or because you will get stronger – but it will get better. You'll find ways to make Cambridge work for you and you will be fine. In fact, you'll be more than fine. You'll make friends for life, you'll leave your mark and eventually, you'll enjoy it.

Behind that letter were two years of navigating the white-dominated spaces of Cambridge, and learning how to survive and thrive in an environment that at times felt as if it had been expressly designed to make life harder for black women. But even before arriving at university, we had been given more than a hint that we weren't going to get an easy ride.

# Introduction

## Chelsea

'*Cheers!*'

One summer night in 2015, I came downstairs to find my dad and five men I had never met before having a party in my dining room: bottles of whisky and schnapps, laughter and a lot of chatter. My dad was celebrating the fact that I had got into the University of Cambridge. It was an important night for my parents. After years of hard work and sacrifice, I had *made it* – for all of us. I poked my head around my dining room door to find out what was going on, and was met with congratulatory applause. I joined the party, was reminded every ten seconds that I shouldn't take the opportunity for granted, and accepted a £50 note from one of the men (thanks uncle). We celebrated what was meant to be the end of something. Really, it was just the beginning.

My mum and dad came to the UK from Ghana during the Margaret Thatcher years with only 70p between them. After moving around in East London for a while, by the time I was born they had made a conscious decision to settle in Chingford, East London (or Essex). In comparison to inner-London's concrete jungles, Chingford was green and leafy, and despite being small, has raised the likes of David Beckham and Blazin' Squad. Growing up as the youngest child, I absorbed influences from all directions. I would sit wedged between my mum and dad eating banku and pepper, trying to follow the Twi that rolled off their tongues. Through them, I developed a strong sense of what it meant to be proud and Ghanaian. From an early age they made sure I never lost my connection with our mother country's food, culture, language or customs. Respect your elders, never use your left hand to receive *anything*, and when you enter a room, always greet people from right to left.

By the time I reached the age of eleven, I had started begging my older brother and sister to take me to garage raves with them. I would wait until they got home from nights out, and screw my face with envy when they both came home late boasting about Jay-Z and

Kanye West's 'Watch the Throne' concert. But once I was old enough to realise that they weren't just being mean siblings and I was actually too young, I saw just how much they were my idols (and still are). I spent the next few years calculating the steps it would take to be *exactly* like both of them. They were both elite athletes, so I planned to be an elite athlete. Jeanette liked house and garage music, so I started listening to house and garage music. Louie studied sports science at Loughborough University, so naturally, I would also do the same.

For as long as I can remember, I've loved the fact that no one could pin down my identity. I never wanted to have one defining characteristic. I wanted people to see that I could be all of them at once. I wanted to be complex, be able to change my mind, have opinions and interests that didn't necessarily make sense all the time. My identity was never just me: it was the perfect distillation of everyone and everything around me.

So when university finally came around, a few weeks after my dad's party, I was excited. Maybe a little bit too excited. I imagined it as the perfect opportunity to explore whether I had any other interests to add to my mélange of a personality. Once I got there, I drank red wine from a cow's horn while shouting Anglo-Saxon phrases to others as part of a college initiation; regularly wore a gown to eat dinner; was hospitalised for a potential heart defect brought on by eating too much pasta; and almost ran over an old lady while learning how to ride a bike on the road.

But throughout my whole experience, something my dad said to me after my first term at Cambridge stuck in my head: '**If I was walking past a bus-stop and I saw you sitting there, I would never believe that you went to Cambridge.**' Still tinged with a sense of disbelief, he never failed to remind me: I still look very young, and there's something about me that doesn't seem quite Cambridge. We both knew that I didn't fit the typical narrative of Oxbridge: privately educated, middle-class and, of course, white. In fact, I was a walking conundrum – black, a woman and working class. My university experience was never going to be 'normal'. There was a constant feeling of being a burden, and that my identity forced people to 'tolerate' or 'accommodate' me. If it wasn't a pity-party for 'poor black students', it was someone attributing all your successes to tick-box quotas.

More than anything, it was a stark reminder that I had no control over my identity. As an eighteen-year-old, it was hard to grapple with the fact that I had entered an environment which meant that I was black before I was anything else. Not only black in being, but black in theory, stereotypes, principle and reality. It would soon become my most defining characteristic, in a place in which I had thought I would have the licence to explore every facet of my identity.

## Ọrẹ

My name is Ọrẹ. Not 'or-ray' or 'or-ee' or 'or'. It's Ọrẹ. With a short 'e', like the first 'e' in elephant.

A teacher at secondary school once told me that she struggled to pronounce my name because it sounded unfinished, like something should come after it. Well, she was half right – my name is actually Oreoluwa Hannah Ngozichukwuka Oluwafunmilayo Ogunbiyi. But I let everyone call me Ọrẹ, as long as they at least *try* to say it right.

I was born in Croydon. I went to school here until I was seven. For my first few years of school, everyone called me 'Or-ee'.

Then my family moved from Croydon to Nigeria. We stayed there for six years. For six years everyone pronounced my name the way my parents did. For once, my name was not something that immediately cast me into an outlier category – if anything, it did quite the opposite. I now knew what it felt like to be part of a norm, and not made to stand out due to my racial and cultural identity.

We moved back to England in 2010, and I told myself that I wouldn't let anyone mispronounce my name any more. I came back surer of who I was, who I am: Ọrẹ and not Or-ee. I had reached a stage where my name was no longer a source of insecurity but one of pride, and a story in itself. But what I couldn't bring back to England with me was that sense of inclusion and normalness that came with being part of a community where almost everyone had long names with deep meanings – more explicitly, where almost everyone was black.

When I moved back, I was black. I came back with a sense of security in my identity as a Yoruba woman, and as a Nigerian woman, but equally, I had to come to terms with what it meant to be black in Britain. I went to a very diverse boarding school, and although I loved it, it fooled me into thinking that everywhere would be just as diverse, just as readily accepting of my Nigerianness, my blackness and all the intricacies that come with those traits. In my final year there, I gave a lecture to the other sixth formers and my teachers on the history of Pan-Africanism, I interviewed the Nigerian Nobel Laureate Wole Soyinka for my school's magazine, and I would spend the weekends cooking Nigerian food in our boarding house kitchen – but at no point did I feel that I was being 'too black'.

University would change that for me. As soon as I accepted my place, I felt the return of the identity crisis that I had not felt since I had reclaimed my name. The closer I got to Cambridge, the clearer it became that my blackness would mediate my university experience. I wish that I had been better prepared for what that would actually mean.

Cambridge put 'being black' into new terms for me. My blackness became something I had to protect, fight for, defend and explain. It isn't news that Cambridge, like most of the UK's other top universities, is particularly white. I was one of three black girls in my year group at Jesus College, a group that comprised some 150 people, and time and time again, black students at other colleges would tell me how lucky I was because they were the only black person that their college had accepted that year. I got used to the questions about 'where I'm from'; and got used to the follow-up question about 'where I'm *really* from'; I got used to the attendant confusion of me saying that I was born in the UK. Being a black girl at Cambridge left me with no hope of blending into the background.

As a minority in a predominantly white space, to take up space is itself an act of resistance.

### Taking Up Space

Regardless of who you are and where you go, your university years are transformative. They are your first taste of independence and they are the beginning of a difficult transition into adulthood. Above all, we're told the *experience* is life-changing: friends for life, venturing out of your comfort zone and learning all the different ways you can cook pasta.

As if university weren't enough of a challenge, navigating university as a black girl is a unique experience, especially when you go to one of the whitest universities in the country (77.1 per cent of the student population identified as white). It wasn't until we met other black women at Cambridge that we realised that we weren't the only ones facing challenges. Despite the fact that we all had different experiences, there was always something that drew us back into the epicentre. Over food, drinks, lots of laughter and genuine company, we felt part of a sisterhood – one that we knew would be unique to the environment that we were in.

So from the beginning, we always wanted *Taking Up Space* to offer that sisterhood: brutally honest whilst reassuring, almost like an older sister telling you what fashion trends to avoid because she's been there and done that. It is now a book laced with personal anecdotes, as well as more general commentary from a wide group of black female and non-binary students on how their identity as black women and students has mediated their experiences of university – with the hope that black girls everywhere will find solace in their stories.

For black girls: understand that your journey through university is unique. Use this book as a guide to help figure out how you want to 'do' university. Our wish for you is that you read this and feel empowered, comforted and validated in every emotion you experience, or decision that you make. For everyone else: we can only hope that reading this helps you to be a better friend, parent, sibling or teacher to black girls living through what we did. It's time we stepped away from seeing this as a problem that black people are charged with solving on their own. It's a collective effort that everyone has a role to play in. The sure result is that our education system will be the better for it, and students of all backgrounds will benefit. The thought of enriched histories, expansive curricula and inclusive environments alone should be enough to spur us all on.

# 1

## *Getting In*
Chelsea

On the way back from my open day at Cambridge's Corpus Christi College, I cried non-stop until I got home.

The University of Cambridge was never on my radar at school; when I heard it mentioned, it was never in reference to me. At the beginning of Year 12, I had narrowly missed out on gaining a place in the 'exclusive' form group made up of a small number of students who got the best GCSE grades and who would receive special help when applying to Oxbridge. Their morning tutor sessions were informative and inquisitive, and exceeded the expectations of the academic curriculum. Most importantly, they would have direct application and interview help. A few steps down the corridor, my form group was debating football teams and haircuts, and planning how to clean up on sports day. I tried to brush it off, pretend that I didn't care about getting into that group, but I was upset. I had worked so hard – only to find out on results day that I was one A* short. My confidence was at an all-time low, and I limited my aspirations from early on.

At the end of Year 12, however, I discovered that I had been predicted A*A*A* for A-levels – the only pupil in my school not in that exclusive form group to receive that prediction. Even at that moment, going to Cambridge seemed like a distant dream: it wasn't expected. Yet I was told by a teacher that if I got to interview stage, my personality would guarantee me a place. I thought about it for a while, and decided I had nothing to lose. It would only be one university choice after all, and I would hate for there to be a niggling voice in the back of my mind constantly asking, 'What if you had applied, and got in?'

So I applied. But I had left it so late that all of the college open days were full, with the exception of one: Corpus Christi College. Without hesitating I submitted my request form. Once the panic was over, I decided to read a bit about the college I was going to visit. I read that Corpus Christi was established in 1352, making it one of the oldest colleges in Cambridge. There was a chapel, courts and a 'Master' of the college, apparently. I read that you weren't allowed to walk on the grass. I laughed. What was this place? I soon fell into a Wikipedia hole reading all about famous Cambridge alumni like Charles Darwin, Stephen Hawking and Prince Charles – not to marvel at them, but to remind myself that I had nothing in common with them.

The day for the visit arrived soon enough. In the morning, I promised myself I wouldn't get too attached, and told myself over and over again, 'If you don't expect anything, you won't be disappointed.' I decided to wear my older sister's blue and pink Aztec blazer from Primark, because I had no smart clothes apart from my sixth form school uniform. I already knew that I wasn't going to get in, so I thought I may as well look cool.

My mum and my brother-in-law drove me up. I was completely overwhelmed by how antiquated, quaint and cobbled everything was. My mum and brother-in-law were packed off with the parents, and I was left with other hopeful applicants. After a small introductory lecture and a tour of the Corpus Christi grounds, I started talking to a girl around my age about our different backgrounds and how nervous we were to apply to Cambridge because it was so competitive. Throughout the open day, we clung to each other, and I remember thinking to myself, 'I can't believe I've made a friend already! Maybe I do actually belong here?' My expectations had been so low that I was shocked to find I was actually having a good time. The staff were friendly, the students were helpful, and the college was very pretty. Chelsea 1 – Cambridge 0!

When my new friend and I split up for our subject-focused workshops, I felt an ounce of confidence. I sat up straight in my chair, eyes bright and ready to contribute. But the feeling didn't last for long. The first applicant introduced himself as 'educated in Surrey with a particular interest in thirteenth-century history', and it was only a short moment before the black cloud of imposter syndrome gathered over my head. My inner self screamed, 'See! These are the people who have *a lot* in common with Darwin, Hawking and Prince Charles. I do not *belong* here.' When it was my turn to introduce myself, I coughed, masked my Essex-London accent, and quietly said that I had a 'particular interest in modern British political history'. I lied. I couldn't believe that I felt so insecure that I had to *lie*. As I listened to everyone else talking eloquently about historical theories and obscure historical figures, I kept quiet. I felt so stupid – but I was even more upset with myself for ever believing that I could fit in here. Chelsea 1 – Cambridge 1.

I was relieved to bump into my new friend after the session. She was beaming as she told me how fun and engaging her workshop had been. I lied, again, and told her that mine was also really fun. By then parents and relatives had arrived back from the family tour. As we approached them, the girl's mum shot me a disgusted look. I smiled, but her expression didn't change. It seemed to say, 'What are you doing here?' – and I'm pretty sure it wasn't directed at my blazer, because Aztec was in fashion then. After staring at me for a good five seconds, she swiftly guided her daughter away without giving us a chance to say goodbye.

I shrank. I was silent on the walk to the car, as my mum told me about all the facts she had learnt about all the other Cambridge colleges. She had had so much fun – how could I possibly tell her that I hated it? That I had already started snowballing lies to fit in? That this was the first time I had been made to feel *other*?

I managed to keep it together at first. But then I got a call from my sister, excitedly asking how it went, and the wailing started. 'I HATE IT SO MUCH,' I sobbed into the car speaker. Once I was able to talk without bursting into tears, I thanked my mum and brother-in-law for coming with me, and told them that they didn't need to worry about me, because I was never going to set foot in Cambridge again.

Chelsea 1 – Cambridge 2.

Game over.

*

Black women are entering higher education in the UK in larger numbers every year. In 2017-18, UK domiciled students who identified as black totalled 77,000 and had the largest gender disparity of any ethnic group with women comprising 59.2 per cent. It is undeniable that there has been a consistent and persistent desire amongst black women to be formally educated.

For me, education was a form of armour, which later would become a strategy of resistance. It was a space in which I could critique frameworks of knowledge and begin my own process of self-actualisation. At fourteen years old, I had made it my mission to learn a little bit about everything after a lesson on *Macbeth* given by a temporary English teacher. Every time we shot him a question, he knew the answer. I wanted to be so smart that there could never be a reason for me to fail. And I truly believed that education was meritocratic: translation, if I worked hard enough, I could be anything that I wanted to be, and no one could stop me. Picture fourteen-year-old me wagging a finger at my older brother in the car: 'They can take your car and your house, Louie, but they can never take your education!' Wise words from such a young soul.

But as Professor of Race and Gender Heidi Mirza states, higher education represents a contradiction for black women. Despite black women wanting to be educated and demonstrating immense will in doing so, our energy is never matched by a corresponding enthusiasm from larger institutions like universities. We're made to believe that we are the problem: underachieving, misunderstood and not 'hardworking' enough. The narrative of meritocracy, which runs through the core of universities, has created a justification for inequality – a dangerous justification, which ignores the intricacies in what it means to be a black woman in higher education.

### Barriers to Entry

Let's start by looking at what shapes the educational choices a lot of black girls make today. A quick flick through an A-level sociology book will tell you that sorting students in bands or sets according to ability is only one of the ways that our education system sets up teacher and pupil relations. Labelling some as 'able' and others as 'less able' can create a self-fulfilling prophecy, in ways that can be detrimental to pupils and their educational futures. Primary and secondary school teachers' expectations can have a lasting impact on their pupils, making some black students feel unable to attend top universities. One of the primary factors in most of us being able to apply to the universities we want to attend is our predicted grades. These predicted grades rest largely on expectations that drive a wedge between those who are deemed deserving or undeserving of 'success'.

Long before the 'exclusive' form group became a possibility, I was picked to be part of a school programme called 'Beyond Horizons', in which a group of 'more able' Year 10 students followed a ten-week programme of Saturday morning sessions. I was chosen for my optimistic attitude to learning, which I was told was seen as a promising mark of early character development. The Saturday morning sessions were actually a lot of fun. We had sessions on critical thinking, learnt a small bit of Cantonese and went on field trips across the country. Through Beyond Horizons, I was given the opportunity to make a lasting impression on school life. I was Head Girl when, during Year 12, the deputy headteacher of my school proudly unveiled a shiny new 'Russell Group' board, which had engraved on it all the names of the students who had got into a Russell Group university, and their chosen subjects.

However, I've come to realise that my secondary school experience was something of an anomaly. It wasn't 'normal' to have teachers rooting for you and your ambitions. Before you even get to the application stage, you will probably find that you're already limited in what you can do. Barbara and I went to the same school, and I remember how upset she was when a few teachers tried to convince her to apply to Oxbridge to do English instead of medicine. Despite volunteering at a surgery and at care homes, and researching medical papers, apparently her skillset pointed to all things English – despite the fact that she repeatedly said she didn't want to study it. We couldn't believe it.

**'Don't do medicine, do English at Oxbridge,' they said . . . I liked English, I liked reading the books and I could write an essay. But I wasn't**

**talented at English to the point where it was like,** *go to Oxbridge.* **– Barbara**

It's easy to believe that your school and teachers know what is best for you – because they're professionals, right? We see them as unquestionably objective and rational in their thinking and advice. But the reality is that teachers can be highly influential in limiting our expectations and ambitions.

**You would think that as teachers, there would be more accountability in ensuring that students reach their potential but oftentimes, they're facilitating and even reinforcing these institutional barriers. – Renée**

Racialised language and tropes all seem to emphasise what black students can *realistically* achieve – especially when applying to university. Most of the ideas about black students originate from a place of authority, with underpredictions of grades explained away as a safe and well-intentioned protection mechanism. But with black Caribbean students three times more likely to be excluded from school than their white counterparts, it is clear that the way parts of the education system are set up disadvantages most black students. Lower expectations for black students have always been simply accepted by parents and students alike, because of the teacher's claim to know our abilities the best. And what remit are we given to challenge those views?

The reality is that teachers of all races – but particularly those who are non-black – are unable to detach their subconscious biases around black students and what we're capable of. It's almost as if we're being trained for specific functions within society. As black women, our ambitions are always capped.

> **I wanted to go to the London School of Economics, and at the time my grades were pretty competitive. I had the references and I was a competitive candidate – but the first thing that [the postgraduate applications advisor] let me know was that it was a difficult school to get into. – Saredo**

> **Even the teachers were like, 'Are you sure that this environment will be conducive for you?' and I was like, 'It's one of the best universities in the world, why wouldn't it be a place for me?' – Renée**

With black girls, there's a fine line between claiming to know what's best for us and deterring us from things that we are genuinely capable of. It's at this cross-roads that you realise that our education system doesn't exist in a vacuum. As Saredo later went on to say, it's as if teachers are '**obsessed with not letting black girls dream**'.

It was only once I arrived at university that I became aware of the possibilities enabled by private schools. I would come to realise that in many ways, these were the students who *had* been given the licence to dream. I went from an environment of not knowing a single soul who went to private school to going to a university so exclusive that they 'recruit more students from eight top schools than almost 3,000 other English state schools put together'. From teaching style to pastoral care and resources, private schooling is a fundamentally different experience – academically and socially. Around 7 per cent of all UK school pupils attend independent schools. Statistics also show that over 50 per cent of GCSE entries from independent schools are awarded a grade A/A*, compared to a national average of 20 per cent.

The difference between private and state schools extends beyond the student, flagging up key differences between the knowledge of teachers and parents as well. It was only on a recent visit back to my secondary school that the annual sixth-form magazine *APPLY* was brought to my attention. I couldn't believe I'd never heard of it. The magazine discusses everything from apprenticeships to current news, and includes almost everything you might need to know about universities.

Crucially, it wasn't just for state-educated students, but also for their parents and teachers, who were unlikely to know much about the university process.

When I first met Ọrẹ, I couldn't help but compare our experiences. At her school, it seemed that every single student was given every chance to flourish academically. Excellence was expected of everybody, not just the few students who performed well in exams. When she reached Year 12, she sat down, as every student did, with her head teacher to discuss her future options. There was also extra help available for all those who expressed an interest in applying for Oxbridge.

**Anyone applying to Oxbridge at my school also had an Oxbridge mentor. – Ọrẹ**

However, Ọrẹ continued and said '**I don't think a lot of people at my school were putting money on me**' to get into Oxbridge. Despite access to resources, networks and financial advantages, it would be wrong to assume that a homogenous experience of private schools exists amongst all students. Kenya went on to say:

'**Having attended a private school for most of my education I'm grateful for everything that it allowed me to achieve but I also think there can be similar patterns of expectations for black**

**students. When I moved to a state school, I definitely felt more encouraged. My experience might not be typical, but I do think it's important to recognise the diversity of experiences for black students even if they are in private schools.'**

For the first time in my life, I was face to face with a real and complex class divide, and struggling to work out what the experiences of black students at private and grammar schools meant for me. To me, it seemed that private schools were always extending a 'helping hand' in the shape of scholarships, charities and trusts to students from minority ethnic backgrounds. Yet since forever, 'black' and 'disadvantaged' had always been in the same sentence.

In reality, there has always been a silent minority of middle-class black students, who have been regularly crammed into the same category of ethnicity in diversity reports. The majority of these students are well-versed on how to navigate white-dominated spaces and assert themselves. While speaking to another black girl who went to my university, but previously attended a prestigious private school in London, she explained to me how she had 'always been told that [she's] the best'. And trust me, she believed it. It's important to stress in plain English that black doesn't always mean working-class. Little has been done to challenge the cultural positioning of black students as a homogenous group, because these conversations, which fail to recognise nuances within our experiences, still persist.

Entering elite institutions that are fundamentally sep-aratist on matters regarding race *and* class is difficult. It only took a few weeks for me to realise that I wasn't able to relate to many of the black students there either. If you type my name into Google, one of the first things to come up is a BBC article entitled 'What it's like being black and working class at Cambridge' (famous, I know). My mum's a cardiology nurse and my dad has worked in a post office depot since I was born. When my mum wanted to study for her nursing degree, my dad made the sacrifice to go part-time because we couldn't afford childcare. Ever since then, money definitely hasn't been in excess. My working class identity, to me, has always been based primarily on my parents' income, and most importantly, how I have chosen to identify. It's not a trend or a fashion statement, but how I and the people around me have navigated through life.

It was only recently that St Hugh's College Student Union in Oxford thought it was appropriate to have a 'Romans and Roadmen' Bop (college party). The description jokingly said: 'pls [sic] do not bring knives or large swords as part of either your roadman or roman costume'. At the height of a knife-crime epidemic that is largely killing young black working-class people, it's beyond me how anyone would even be able to write something like that – just to be 'edgy' and cool. Within hours, the sentence was swiftly deleted and replaced with a *Dazed* article entitled 'How to culturally appreciate and not culturally appropriate'.

I realise that for some of you reading this, class inequality may be a more present and pressing issue than race. Many people aren't able to simply take for granted the ability to pay the £24 UCAS fee (or £60 per university for a Master's application), access to the internet and parental buy-in to our education. They might yelp to learn that on average, a university student in the UK receives around £3,000 from their parents a year. In particular, Durham University students received on average around £500 a month from their beloved parents.

Even though the Bank of Mum and Dad can be nice, parents are above all seen as playing a vital part in our educational attainment. Parents and carers are our 'first teachers', helping us navigate through school and pre-university choices. Some parents take an interest not only in the behavioural attitudes of their children but also in developing skills, school policy and organisation.

**I remember the lecturer saying, 'Children from middle-class families are usually read to every**

**night just like your parents would have,' and that was my first taste of Imposter syndrome because I was like, 'Wow, OK. Like, not only should I be middle class, but I should have two parents – and if I don't fit that criteria, should I even be here?' – Eireann**

For the majority of black children, parental buy-in to educational development is complicated by matters of race and class. From languages and accents which provoke racial assumptions to unfamiliarity with the UK's education system, studies all point to the fact that the majority of black parents are at a disadvantage when it comes to parental engagement. Reni Eddo-Lodge sums this up perfectly in *Why I'm No Longer Talking to White People About Race* when talking about the intersection between race, class and expectations:

**Children of immigrants are often assured by well-meaning parents that educational access to the middle classes can absolve them from racism. We are told to work hard, go to a good university, and get a good job.**

My parents' work schedules meant that they did not have the time to support and supplement my education. This is true of many parents. My mum and dad were always excited when I came home beaming with my end of term report, but they couldn't invest in my education in the way that they might have liked to. Parents' and information evenings, for example, almost always clashed with my mum's night shifts and my dad's late shifts. Luckily for me, my older brother and sister would step in as my parent-designates for the night. For working-class students and our parents alike, educational attainment becomes a mechanism whereby we can escape the cycle of poverty when given an opportunity to. The Sutton Trust found that some groups, including black Africans, appear to have higher levels of aspiration than others, with pupils showing greater interest in schooling, despite relatively high levels of poverty and being more likely to have free school meals.

**My mind was elsewhere. My mum had been diagnosed with a blood clot and she couldn't work so my stress was that I need to go to work and I'm in school. Who's going to provide for me? Who's going to provide for my family? – Courtney**

In such an environment, you don't have the luxury of time, or the luxury to prioritise your own development – financial matters are much more pressing. Before applying to university, the prospect of a huge student debt was a massive put-off that made me seriously question whether it was worth it. I couldn't see the fairness in my brother and sister only paying £3,000 a year while I was made to buck the cost of a £9,000 bill. Worst of all, they were *still* paying off their loans, so I pretty much imagined myself going to the grave with my debt. But one day I saw Martin Lewis, the MoneySavingExpert. com founder, on TV, successfully 'myth-busting' student loans. He explained so many things that I wished I could have known for myself and shared with some of my friends, who thought that the debt wasn't worth it. For example, after thirty years any and all remaining debt is wiped. Many people who earn under £25,000 are unlikely to pay it all back within thirty years anyway. Furthermore, I had no idea about all the scholarships and bursaries that I was eligible for. Nowadays, I'd sadly describe my relationship with student finance as like having a temporary boyfriend – you get excited every time you get that occasional text: *Your money will arrive in your Bank Account within three working days*. But when you break up for good, you get hit with a massive bill asking you for everything he gave you back. I know. It's tragic.

If you're a black girl who is working-class, you'll understand that the relationship between class and race is far from simple. Moreover, when speaking to Nathania, who's from Manchester, it dawned on me how ignorant I had been about the huge discrepancies between regions across the UK. For example, in Northern Ireland, black ethnic groups make up less than 0.1% of the population meaning that whilst almost all of the students in North-ern Ireland are white, less than half in London are. Regional disparities serve to highlight the vast gulf of inequality between black students who live anywhere other than the capital and those in London. If you're a black student who's grown up *outside* London, you're probably familiar with being overlooked in conversations to do with access. Most access events that focus specifically on black working-class students happen in London, or in partnership with schools in inner-city London. That means if you're from the north of England, you'll realistically have to travel down on an £80 ticket for an event that might last for only two or three hours. Unfortunately, this results in a bit of a paradox: an access barrier to access.

Add to this the very real prejudice against regional accents, which are often associated with negative aspects of being working-class. Nathania, now in her third year at Trinity College, Cambridge, felt that people immediately formed a negative impression of her simply because of her accent, automatically questioning her right to attend an elite academic institution, and contributing to her struggle to 'fit in':

**I think it's a lot to do with my [Mancunian] accent. People just presume that I haven't got a brain.**

The intersection of class and region can be a huge deterrent to following your desired path. But crucially, recognising this at least puts you on a stronger footing to find a way to plan and confront these issues in the best way possible.

*

When applying to university, one 'deal-breaker' for me was culture. Academic credentials aside, I was eager to find somewhere that had at least some remnants of the culture I knew and loved in London – somewhere with food markets where I could buy plantain, places to get my braids done, and some diversity in the local population. So . . . I planned to apply to only London universities. Call it regional privilege, maybe, but I didn't know anywhere else, and London for me was a safe bet. I grew up in and around the city. It was my home. To be completely honest, the thought of leaving it scared me. The three universities with the biggest black student populations are all in London: London Metropolitan, the University of East London and the University of West London, where black students make up more than a third of all first-year undergraduates. After students from Bangladeshi backgrounds, black Caribbean students are most concentrated in the most diverse universities, which have tended to be in London or Birmingham. Young black Londoners have *created* a culture through music, dance and language that is so specific to London that it would be hard to imagine yourself anywhere else.

A lack of relatable culture at university has a direct correlation with the drop-out rates of black students. The University Partnerships Programme Foundation and Social Market Foundation found that more than one in ten (10.3 per cent) black students drop out of university, in comparison with 6.9 per cent of the whole student population. I was not surprised to read that the main factors were 'lack of cultural connection to the curriculum' and difficulty in making friends with students from other ethnicities. This isn't to assume that all black people are likely to be friends – but going to a university where hardly anyone looks like you signifies a massive problem. You feel as if every single other black student knew something that you didn't, and that's why none of them are here. You might begin to question whether you could be happier somewhere else (or even not in higher education at all).

It becomes a self-perpetuating choice to pick a university that you know other black students will be at, regardless of whether it's a top one. This has led some to claim a form of 'self-segregation' due to lack of 'ethnic mixing' in the UK's universities, in terms not only of the student body but also academics, support staff and culture. This creates a system in which white middle class students go to certain universities, and poor ethnic minority students go to others. Universities like these which are more ethnically diverse tend to be 'less wealthy universities which provide higher education for large numbers of first-generation university students'. Moreover, universities in ethnically diverse cities attract an ethnically diverse student body. That in turn encourages greater diversity. The student population of Coventry University, for example, is 54.5 per cent white and 44.5 per cent BME. From the outset, there's strength in numbers.

With the retention of black students at an all-time low, being selective about university choices becomes a mechanism for insulating yourself from entering institutions that aren't looking out for your best interests. You even get to skip the feeling that your presence is just another way of ticking a few boxes. Instead, there's comfort in being surrounded by other black students – more so than in choosing the 'best' universities.

## School of Institutional Racism

Professor David Gillborn, Director of the Centre for Research in Race and Education at the University of Birmingham, believes that England's education system is home to 'insidious institutionalised racism'. And he's right. Institutional racism can be defined as the collective failure of an organisation or institution to provide the appropriate framework for people because of their colour, culture or ethnic origin. From attitudes and behaviours to ignorance and racist stereotyping, all processes work to systematically disadvantage minority ethnic people. Black students have to work to identify and highlight subtle forms of racism that operate against the common belief that racism is easily recognisable. This very fact is what makes the institutionalisation of racism within our education system so insidious. It's easy to deny when it's woven in with privilege and power.

In 2018, the *Independent* reported on data which revealed that black students are twenty-two times more likely to have their university applications investigated for possible fraudulent activity. The UK-based organisation dealing with the application process for British universities, UCAS, claims it is 'at the heart of connecting people to higher education'. However, between

2013 and 2017, a Freedom of Information request found that the applications of 2,675 black British undergraduate applicants were flagged in comparison to 995 white British applicants. In response to the criticism, UCAS attributed blame to the fraud detection software it uses to screen applications, which 'uses historical data as a reference'.

The UCAS example is at the crux of why institutional racism has managed to persist today. Institutional racism is faceless – by which I mean, the individual motive of racism is removed from the institution, resulting in depersonalisation. How can an *institution* possibly be racist? As students, we're left fighting a system within which no one person or institution is willing to admit to their failures. Instead, we're directed to failings of 'systems' and 'operations' as a way of rationalising it.

In 2015, the number of black students accepted by Russell Group universities stood at 2,740. Before you ask: yes, this is comparatively low. Yet a BBC 'Reality Check' article, including 'five charts that tell the story of diversity in UK universities', said: 'Black and minority ethnic students of all backgrounds are actually punching above their weight when it comes to representation at university.' Black students make up 8 per cent of the UK university population, despite accounting for 4 per cent of young people aged eighteen to twenty-four in

England and Wales. However, this 'overrepresentation' is not reflected within the UK's redbrick universities (typically regarded as the top institutions).

Every so often, a headline about the underrepresentation of black students in elite academic institutions rears its ugly head in national news. Around every six months, it seems as though every major newspaper has an alarm set. During my time at Cambridge, those moments were the worst. Journalists flooded your inboxes on every social media site. All the black students became hyper-visible, and all the white students were reminded to pity you and exclaim that they 'didn't know you were the *only* one!' – despite facing that fact every day. Or, my personal favourite, being constantly asked, 'Are you sure the lack of diversity at Oxbridge is not because black students aren't applying?' Probably. But have you ever thought to question *why* they're not applying? The journalists who write these stories continue to have no regard for the black students who are actually in these institutions. These very stories also have an effect on our experiences at university. It's exhausting.

As it stands, the decentralised administration system at Oxbridge falters when it comes to access and outreach. It turns it into a game of who can get more black students into their universities, so that they can avoid the tabloids. Despite a genuine commitment from some school liaison officers and access staff, this rat race actually overlooks inclusion issues, such as how welcome black students feel on university grounds once they arrive. Universities view themselves as liberal and progressive places that are at the forefront of society. Formal education is still believed to be a sure means of gaining that social mobility passport. Clinging on to this vision of what our educational system *could* be, universities are prone to ignoring the fact that racism can still be at the core of the same institution that is offering platforms to discuss and learn about it.

The challenge universities now face is addressing an access problem under constant scrutiny. Here lurks the word 'diversity', which has become a catch-all cliché – one that points to inclusivity and representation, without ever taking in what it really *means*. Let's take the strategic objectives from the University of York's Equality, Diversity and Inclusion Strategy 2017-2022:

- Objective 1: Embed equality into all aspects of university life.

- Objective 2: Attract, attain and succeed.

- Objective 3: Be flexible and adaptive to the needs of our diverse university community.

- Objective 4: Adopt an inclusive campus approach.

I searched. And searched. I wanted to make sure that the above hadn't really been published as an equality, diversity *and* inclusion scheme that was supposed to span five years? There is no strategy within the report, no mention of *how* the university would 'monitor and address differences in degree outcomes', or *how* the university would be committed to 'promoting a culture based on the principles of respect, dignity and inclusion'. If you think I'm being harsh, have a look at SOAS University of London's Equality, Diversity and Inclusion Strategy (2016-2020). Its report not only includes detailed and specific strategic objectives for 2016-2020, but individual stories of students who are most affected by 'diversity and inclusion' policies. Most importantly, the ways in which progress will be measured and maintained. Point 10, 'Ensuring Progress', demonstrates the sophistication of acknowledging that as staff and students, we all serve different roles and responsibilities when it comes to these issues. Rather than suggesting a widespread commitment to 'equality', there is an understanding that Diversity and Inclusion Managers have a fundamentally different role to the Board of Trustees. By pinpointing specific groups, this at least ensures a standardised and coherent commitment to strategic objectives.

It seems as if most universities are stringing sentences together in an attempt to prove that they are doing something – *anything*. We're left with vague strategic papers that lack critique, discussion and direction. Sadly, it's the students who fall under the 'diverse' umbrella who suffer when universities send a clear message that equality is an afterthought.

The Racial Equality Charter (REC) is just one example of a 'gold star' sticker system that has been put in place for institutions. The REC aims to improve the 'representation, progression and success of minority ethnic staff and students within higher education'. A report by Professor Kalwant Bhopal and Clare Pitkin, detailing the experiences of the individuals responsible for the implementation of the REC in their institutions, found that all interviewees welcomed the REC. However, many felt that institutions were slow to respond to the fact that additional resources needed to be invested 'to provide adequate provision and support when applying for the REC'. I wasn't surprised to learn that institutions could be deemed as 'proactive and working towards the REC' while still employing staff who demonstrated negative attitudes towards BME students.

Oxford and Cambridge are both universities that are regularly associated with elitism, bastions of social privilege that groom the future leaders of today. In particular, Labour MP for Tottenham David Lammy has been persistent in challenging Oxbridge to admit to and rectify its diversity problem. In 2016, 1.5 per cent of the Cambridge intake was black and 1.2 per cent of the intake at Oxford, according to the Higher Education

Statistics Agency. In response to Lammy's criticisms, Professor Graham Virgo, Pro-Vice-Chancellor for Education at Cambridge, together with senior colleagues from the Admissions Office, published an open letter addressing diversity in admissions. The letter stated that Cambridge had admitted fifty-eight black students in 2017, representing 33 per cent of all black students admitted to higher education in the UK that year who had attained A*A*A at A-level. But if we're playing the numbers game, how many of those black students went to private school or high-performing grammar schools? Or, how many were based in London? More pressing, how many of those students come from international schools? In the absence of answers, it's difficult not to feel that statistics may have been interpreted to present a 'not-that-bad picture'. What we do know though is that the careful placing of statistics can do much to damage and distort facts.

The current standard of black representation at Oxbridge is not something to be celebrated. At times, black students are met with hostility from other Oxbridge students when we try to do our own bit for access and inclusion. Most notably, when BME students call for a BME representative on a college union, some colleges' voting systems mean that students who *do not* identify as BME have a significant hand in deciding whether a BME officer is 'needed' – often voting the motion down.

At Pembroke College, a BME student created and submitted a proposal for a 'White Majority Ethnic' officer, satirising the arguments that a BME officer patronises, infantilises and ghettoises BME students. It read:

**How could people who come from Three Different Continents AND then some more, be categorised in this manner? How could someone who might refer to home (or homes) located in Adelaide or Middlesbrough, Johannesburg or Minneapolis, Rio de Janeiro or Zurich, stand to represent the struggles and the grievances of the entire WME community?**

Yep. Some people have a *lot* of time on their hands.

Conversations surrounding Oxbridge can be entirely regressive. The two universities nonchalantly claim to be strongholds of excellence and exceptional standards. Yet in the same sentence, they can allude to black students as not achieving *enough* – suggesting that we don't meet those standards of excellence. This isn't a conversation that is happening in isolation. It's something that parents see, prospective black students see, and current black students understand.

**As a black student, you're being seen as someone who's really taking a stand on diversity. But**

**middle-class white people are not the only audience. You have kids that are interested in going to Oxbridge, who are watching and reading these things and thinking, 'Wow, there's only one black student in, I don't know, Worcester College. I'm definitely not applying to Oxford'. You're perpetuating the same system. – Renée**

Renée Kapuku, former President of the University of Oxford's African and Caribbean Society (ACS), has been a trailblazer in disrupting the narrative that Oxbridge isn't for black students. She has been involved in several student-led and some university-supported access and outreach programmes. Oxford ACS's Annual Access Conference is the UK's largest higher education access conference for African and Caribbean students. The conference has a specific focus on black state-school students from disadvantaged backgrounds, and aims to deconstruct Oxford stereotypes through a 'highly personalised social lens'. Since the ACS developed its access framework, applications from black students to Oxford have increased by 24.1 per cent. Clearly, there is strength in having something communicated by someone who looks like you – no glamorisation or sugar-coating, just honesty.

**It's students doing this work where the university is falling short. – Ọrẹ**

As black women, we're never afforded complexity in these narratives about black underrepresentation. Our voices are left outside the conversation. Access is more than trying to pump us in as fast as possible; there has been a lack of nuance and practical suggestions for change. It's always been, 'You're not doing enough,' and never a question of, 'What can we do? How can we help you?' As Renée writes for the Huffington Post, we as black students are 'turned into poor caricatures of the quintessential "black student experience" condensed into one of suffering, strife and "social apartheid"'. Black students taking hold of this narrative regarding access and race is a chance for us to demonstrate that our experiences at elite institutions are far from monolithic. They're colourful and unique.

## Where Do We Go from Here?

I'm definitely not qualified to be the next Minister of Education. However, having spent most of my life in full-time education (seventeen years, to be exact), believe it or not, my experiences have taught me, and the others in this book, a few things about our educational system: some negative and positive, but crucially, all *very* different, stemming from the ways in which we have experienced and tackled institutional racism within various higher education institutions.

Universities are currently run like businesses, with marketisation increasing the role of the student as a consumer: you pay a certain amount, and you expect to leave with a solid grade and a job six months post-graduation. From league table positioning to student satisfaction surveys, it's easy to see this part of marketisation as a form of educational expansion, and potentially a means of reducing inequality by providing more opportunities for people from disadvantaged backgrounds. But the fallout of this is huge.

At present, there is a wide disparity between how much we talk about diversity and how much actual change is happening. Universities have become sophisticated in non-performative 'institutional speech acts' which make commitments to diversity and 'equality'. Your institution may claim to be driving racial equality – while your everyday interactions are telling you something *very* different. Ultimately, the question remains as to whether we can really label an institution as more 'diverse' if its commitment to racial equality is based on the meeting of racial equality targets, rather than listening to the lived experiences of its black students.

So, what can we do?

**I think people who aren't part of these [racial] groups should be equally concerned and giving a helping hand. – Eireann**

The proactiveness of black students on the ground has meant more BME-specific targeting when it comes to matters regarding access before and within university. Bristol Student Union BME network, for example, has created its own influential platform through leading its own discussions and campaigns on topics such as intersectionality, religion and mental health. Without the persistent and collective drive of student labour and voices, I am sure little would be done to change the current status quo of ensuring black students feel integrated before and within the university environment.

Oxford and Cambridge have also both partnered with Target Oxbridge, a free programme which takes on 160 black African and Caribbean students in Year 12 who want help with their applications to the two universities, and provides more opportunities for prospective black students to speak to and ask questions of black students who are already at Oxbridge. The first event I ever went to in Cambridge was hosted by the founder of Target Oxbridge, Naomi Kellman. Target Oxbridge's partnership with both universities has proved to be invaluable in demystifying Oxbridge life.

However, it's clear that methods of tackling inequality and racial disparity within education are still mostly outsourced. Universities are more likely to work with organisations such as Target Oxbridge, Sponsors for Educational Opportunity, IntoUniversity or Future Leaders as a way of fulfilling their diversity pledges. They offload their responsibilities to tackle systemic inequalities within their institutions to privately-run, non-governmental organisations as a tokenistic means of making 'progress', without properly addressing the root causes of these inequalities within their walls.

To some, outsourcing may seem to be a step in the right direction, showing through financial investment and a reliance on experienced organisations a real and specific commitment to rectifying inequalities. Providing a platform for these organisations is also a way of allowing professionals who understand and are black themselves to address specific black issues. But I question the authenticity of many of these diversity schemes.

It's easier to adopt the argument that black students are making conscious choices when navigating the higher education landscape than to ask: *why*? Why are black students 'self-segregating'? Why do we feel a sense of Imposter syndrome before we've even started our university applications? Why do we cry in the car on our way home from open days? Why do we still feel the need to drop out of universities because we don't feel welcome? These questions require *practical* answers – answers that don't start or end with black students, but with the institutions in which they are struggling.

It would be misleading to claim that I have all the answers. I am no expert. I have just about scratched the surface of why so many black girls fail to apply to university, and what awaits them if they do. Most importantly, I can only hope my experiences, and those of others in this book, can colour the conversation on access into – and whilst at – university. If nothing else, foregrounding the lived experiences of black university students paints a more complex picture. It also highlights the fact that there is not one single factor producing the profound gendered and racialised inequalities within our higher education system, but many.

Cambridge may have won on my open day. But I didn't stop playing. By October of that year, I was driving back up to the city again, but this time with all my stuff, ready to move in to my college. Cambridge would score a few more goals over the next year, but it was one of the best decisions I would ever make.

# 2

# #AcademiaSoWhite

## Ọrẹ

As the UK's national curriculum currently stands, it is possible to go through education without encountering Africa at all. The history curriculum, for example, groups 'non-European societies' in a way that encourages them to be viewed as homogenous despite their diverse characters. As a result, students are taught to view the world through a lens of Europe and 'the rest'. Primary schools are only required to look at one non-European society, and the early secondary school curriculum does little to improve on this, despite its aims to teach 'local, regional and international history'. Although universities in the UK have autonomy over how their curricula are set, it is no surprise that their history curricula rarely do a better job than our national curriculum of looking beyond the centrality of European history.

The implications of this whiteness and Eurocentrism go beyond history. This state of affairs mediates our whole educational experiences considerably, so much so that attempting to study anything outside of the white and Eurocentric requires going the extra mile. The contents of the British curriculum have implications for classrooms far beyond the UK, and affect more broadly what is considered to be worthy of academic study. I first became aware of the power of curricula around Year 7. I was in secondary school in Nigeria, and we had spent most of our history lessons that year learning about the Battle of Hastings and the struggles that led up to it – instead of any Nigerian or West African history. It's possible to be in a Nigerian classroom, and yet have your curriculum dictated by powers almost 5,000 miles away.

Inevitably, moving back to England meant that I would only face this curriculum even more directly. After years of learning extensively about the World Wars, I had still had no lessons on the transatlantic slave trade or the colonisation of African states. It became clear that I wasn't going to get a diverse learning experience from my school's curriculum, and that I would have to seek out the extra knowledge on my own. I hoped that going to university would change that.

At my Cambridge interview for human, social and political sciences (HSPS), my red-orange blazer – and my race – were not the only things that made me stand out. All the interviewees for HSPS sat in one room, and around a table there were about five other applicants reading the exact same neon-green politics book. I panicked – I had never, ever seen this book that they all seemed to be really familiar with. I asked someone to see what was inside (even though I really should have been minding my own business, if we're being honest); it was filled with predominantly British political history that I hadn't come across, especially since I didn't even study history at GCSE. There were things inside about the Concert of Europe and Clement Attlee that I knew I could only waffle about for a minute at best. Instead, I went back to my corner of the room and re-read Frantz Fanon's *The Wretched of the Earth* and the pile of JSTOR articles on Pan-Africanism, Kwame Nkrumah and the Négritude that I had been mulling over for the past few months. I hadn't even started Cambridge yet but *that* was when the imposter syndrome kicked in for me. My experiences and my existence felt at odds with the university as a physical space, and as an intellectual one too.

In my first interview, I was asked what I thought was the most significant event of the twentieth century. I stopped and thought: *she must want me to say something like the Second World War.* I had let that stupid green politics book get to me and make me doubt myself. But I paused, and remembered the advice that I had received from my mentor to always steer the question to my strengths. I knew nothing about the Second World War. I did, however, know a lot about the wave of decolonisation that came after it. For me, the fact that a post-war wave of self-determination enabled about one third of the world to ramp up the struggles for their independence, was *way* more significant than a war that I personally felt quite disconnected from.

In my second interview, I was given a piece to read by Isaiah Berlin, discussing the conflict between politics as an art and politics as a science. Based on this, I was asked to decide who Berlin might consider a good leader. The piece had mentioned Otto von Bismarck numerous times and so I felt that if there was a right answer, it had to be him. But again, I had no clue who he was. So I said, 'Well, I know who Berlin might consider a *bad* leader.' I proceeded to talk about how Nkrumah had an understanding of what politics was as a science, but his failure to marry this with the 'art' of politics and apply it to the contentious geopolitical context of the Cold War would make someone like Berlin consider him a bad political leader. I had no idea how that would play out, but I had no choice but to focus on what I knew: the histories that felt close to me, the histories that I could relate to.

It felt like a risky decision, but luckily it paid off. However, the constant struggle of trying to fit my interests, experiences and history into a degree which wasn't always so accommodating was something I grappled with for my whole time at university.

**I was reconciling the parts of my identity that I thought were othered, and I came to understand that being othered is not necessarily a disadvantage but your superpower. – Renée**

Renée puts it best, but it wasn't easy. I didn't just feel like an imposter because I was black in this predominantly white university; I also felt excluded by the nature of my experiences, and in turn, the interests that had developed from those experiences. Histories like mine, and those to which I can more easily relate, are absent on curricula everywhere.

The experience of confronting curricula that don't do enough to acknowledge our experiences as black girls is othering. This experience has its inception in our national curriculum, and has implications for the subjects we choose to study, how we interact (or don't) with our university lectures, and eventually, how well we perform by the end of our degrees. We are dealing with a black attainment gap at university level that doesn't correlate with how well black students perform at GCSE stage, and the lack of black academics at professorial level is at crisis point.

In anticipation of the critics who will say that we are liberal snowflakes complaining about an issue that isn't there, or that this is about black students asking for 'special treatment', I am packing this chapter with data, figures and research that prove that the issue of whiteness in academia is not one that I've constructed in my imagination.

**I think we feel a lot of pressure that we have to produce some kind of evidence as to why you feel marginalised, or some sort of statistical data. But if you feel some type of way, it's truth on its own. Your feelings are its own truth. – Saredo**

But the burden of proof shouldn't be on us. The idea that black students have to go further to show that their experiences are real is recurrent in academic spaces, and this chapter reveals similar issues. Our experiences of grappling with the whiteness in academia are valid, and highlight how black students are being failed by the education system.

## Subjects

Black students make up 7 per cent of the UK university population. However, they are not evenly distributed in proportion across all subjects. Only 2.4 per cent of students who study history are black; the proportion is about 3 per cent for languages, and 5 per cent for the creative arts. To understand why this may be the case, we have to look further back, to the motivations behind our subject choices.

For many students, being attracted to a curriculum is why you might choose to study a particular subject, or even go to a particular university. But most ethnic minority students are thinking about more than just the subject and its content when we choose what to study.

**When you think of English, what are you thinking of? Is it not middle-class white people? – Mikai**

I agree with Mikai. However, I don't think it's because only middle-class white people are good at English, but more because English is a degree that does not have an obvious career path attached to it, and so isn't an obvious choice for those going to university for the sole purpose of improving their career prospects. Being able to study whatever you want without having to think ahead to what careers it might set you up for is a privilege that few have. There are all sorts of challenges and obstacles in the job market for black women, so from as early on as A-levels, you find yourself wanting to study something that seems safe – something that will guarantee stability and security in a society where those things don't come easily. The pressures of a job market that seems to consider some degrees more marketable than others kick in while we choose what to study at university – and in the end, degrees such as English, history, modern languages and the creative arts suffer for it.

Even if we aren't thinking along these lines, our parents are. By the time I approached Year 12, my dad had made it clear that he thought it would be a good idea for me to study law. At one point in my life, I thought a law degree was a good idea too. I regularly watched *Suits* and *The Good Wife* with my mum, and being that kind of corporate lawyer seemed, at that time, to be so *me*. I loved arguing. I debated throughout my secondary school career, and although I took maths, French, politics and economics at A-level, I was clearly tending towards the humanities. I wasn't doing medicine, that was for sure; I had no interest in doing economics either, and so law was the only other vocational-ish degree left. My whole career was planned out: I would study law at Cambridge, qualify in the UK, work in corporate law for a bit. Then I would move back to Nigeria, become a qualified lawyer there, practise for ten years and become a Senior Advocate of Nigeria, something akin to being a Queen's Counsel. But a two-week summer school and a bit of research made me realise that I had zero interest in the law, and that in fact, I loved politics. I had to come home and tell my dad that I wanted to apply for HSPS at Cambridge, a course that felt perfectly curated for me and my broad range of interests, in a way that law wasn't. I told him I would (possibly) do a law conversion once I graduated. (I later abandoned that mission.)

Being relatively privileged in terms of class meant that my experience was slightly different to the norm. My mum went to university, and my dad is an academic (and many of his best friends are too). My challenge was not that I lacked role models, or that my parents didn't appreciate the value of a university degree. The problem was that, in *spite* of my parents' backgrounds, my dad still felt that for me to get my foot in the door as a black woman in today's world, I needed a vocational degree – specifically, a law degree. As I write this, I'm currently doing a master's in journalism at Columbia University in New York. Even now, my dad *still* thinks it would be a good idea for me to go to law school!

I know that my dad's position comes from a place of love and that he only wants the best for me, but I'm also glad that I found the courage to defend my interests and my strengths. Many of my friends were not so fortunate, and have ended up graduating with degrees (a lot of them law degrees) that they are unsatisfied with because they were literally forced to do them by their parents. Over 10 per cent of students who study law in the UK are black, and that's great. While I'm sure that many of them have a genuine love for the law, I have no doubt that equally, many of them are in the same boat that I almost was, studying a degree that they hope will please their parents, and land them a job straight after graduation and, hopefully, financial security.

The role of financial incentives in choosing to study particular subjects at university should not be underestimated. According to research by the Resolution Foundation, black African graduates are twice as likely to work in low-paying occupations as Indian, Chinese and white graduates. We know that the odds are against us, and so we hedge our bets in the hope that the qualification will lead directly to a higher-paying job, so that we don't become part of that damning statistic.

But if you are going to go to university and endure three, four or even six years of excruciating hard work and general stress, you owe it to yourself to choose a degree that you love. You may have parents who are paying for your degree and think that as a result, they have a say in what you study. Yet you are entitled to freedom in that choice. Any degree you earn is meant to teach you transferable skills that can be applied to a whole host of jobs. This might take some extra explaining to your parents, who may not see that now, but you don't have to do a whole law degree to be a lawyer, or politics to be a politician. What makes you scream? What makes you angry? What excites you? What keeps you up at night? What do you want to rant about for hours on end? For me, it wasn't law. I wanted to study a degree that would let me be myself, explore my diverse range of interests, and make me a more rounded person; I found that in HSPS.

HSPS is one of Cambridge's more diverse courses, and I am grateful for that, don't get me wrong. Nevertheless, that's still not saying very much – it just means it's slightly less shocking than the others. In my first year, I studied politics, international relations, sociology and social anthropology. In politics, I learned about what felt like all the white men under the sun, and then I had one lecture on Gandhi (without any mention of his history of anti-blackness, of course, but I digress). The only political theorists that were considered worthy of academic critique, according to my curriculum, were white. Although the course has now changed, my international relations course at the time involved a whole lecture on industrialisation that made no mention of slavery. Someone, somewhere decided that students at one of the world's best universities could accurately study Britain's industrial revolution without acknowledging that it was built off the backs of slaves. International relations, in addition to its theoretical aspects, should also address difficult questions about who does and does not benefit from the ideas and ideologies that dominate our international system. But in this regard, my course sometimes fell short.

Then there is social anthropology. The whole idea of the subject revolves around white 'explorers' studying black and brown people, and I struggled with that as a notion. In these lectures, non-European people are conveyed as something to gawk at, a mysterious subject of intrigue. That objectification made me uncomfortable.

**Anthropology as a whole has a really colonial, negative, horrifying history, and I think that the fact that the people who propagated that are still at the top of the reading lists is incredibly unnecessary. There are amazing anthropologists who are either not those people, or who are actually black and brown anthropologists who have greater cultural respect, and also still fully understand the ideas of [celebrated anthropologists] like Lévi-Strauss and Malinowski. Reading**

**the word 'savage' in Lévi-Strauss's work a hundred thousand times is not the way that I want to spend my time at university. – Saskia**

If you choose to study a humanities subject at university, there are high chances that you're going to be forced to work within the confines of a very white curriculum. Your histories, where they do appear on curricula, will be add-ons, or thrown into collective 'liberation' lectures as afterthoughts. The problem of the white, Eurocentric curriculum isn't unique to HSPS.

**The Cambridge curriculum for English is very Eurocentric, very canonical . . . English at Cambridge was very white, very dry and very non-political. – Arenike**

Although curricula are normally set by senior faculty staff within universities, the 'literary canon' is a set of texts that scholars across the world have effectively agreed are great and special. It typically includes the works of Shakespeare, Homer, a couple of Brontë sisters, and so on, and consists of mostly white, European, male writers. It's presented as an objective list, and is said to be 'representative' of a period. But we have to challenge who gets to decide what is considered 'great' enough to be included in the literary canon, and the conditions under which these kinds of decisions are made. We have to challenge which writers are privileged enough to have their works memorialised in this magical way. Who are the gatekeepers?

On further interrogation, it's clear that the canon is not objective at all. The books that it includes are meant to be 'authoritative' – and therefore end up aligning with socio-political ideas of the time about who could and could not have authority. The early dictators of the canon were white clergymen in the nineteenth century and beyond. Black people were largely not in positions that granted access to education, let alone able to have their works considered worthy of being canonised. This same power dynamic still exists, and as such, the canon hardly includes writers who look like me. The idea that black writers haven't written works great enough to be included in the canon is a myth that is used to justify and perpetuate their exclusion. Cambridge's *Varsity* newspaper featured a 'Rethinking the canon' column by Jonathan Chan that makes a lot of headway in grappling with the issue of the rigidity of the literary canon. But this is not just a university thing. The literary canon is a body of literature that is presented as universal, and is the basis for English curricula across the world and at all levels. You're probably going to study more Brontë sisters than black women in your academic lifetime. That is a problem for everyone.

**It's almost as if these African and black writers were a side dish to the main meal as opposed to really exploring their own work critically. – Saredo**

Chelsea studied history. In her first year, there were ten British history papers, six European history papers, one on empires and world history, and one on 'World' history:

**[On the world history paper] there would be one lecture on Africa, one lecture on Asia, one lecture on Latin America, but then you would have British history, which would be broken down into different areas. It was very specific when it came to European history and British history. – Chelsea**

In studying British history and the atrocities of its empire, we must study more than white and European histories, and we must study them in full. But even for the departments that have acknowledged this need, and gradually introduced the histories of non-white people to their curricula, the topics are obsessively centred around slavery and colonisation. For example, we may discuss the economics of slavery and the role of William Wilberforce in its eventual abolition, or we may speak of former colonies only in terms of their viability for European metropoles. This suggests that non-white people are only worth studying for the occasions in which they are forced to confront white power. But why? Slaves were people before they were enslaved. Black people have existed in history in roles other than those of slaves and subjects of colonialism, but you probably won't get that from your textbooks.

**The [history] curriculum is so dehumanising for black people. It's really othering. – Nathania**

The only times you might see someone who looks like you represented in your curriculum will be at the mention of slavery, colonisation, lynching and maybe political corruption in African states – a dehumanising experience. It is hard to believe that heads of departments think about, or care to think about, what that does to our psyches as black people. Our history books glorify the very people who profited from our exploitation. If we are told in Year 4 that Winston Churchill 'won the war', we should be reminded in the same breath that he was also, as suggested by some, a genocidal racist – given that he was largely responsible for the deaths of some 3 million people during the 1943 Bengal famine. If we're taught about Auschwitz and Nazi concentration camps, we should also be reminded that concentration camps were a tactic first used by the British in the Second Boer War and later against the

Mau Mau in Kenya. How can a university truly pride itself on being at the forefront of knowledge production when the only ideas and theories that they consider worthy of study are white and European, and most likely, propagated by men?

We struggle to find room for our identities in both our curricula and the lectures that stem from them, and that's something that affects black people in a unique way. Lecturers have a duty to be sensitive to that, too. The use of photographs of Ku Klux Klan lynchings in a history lecture could be triggering for black students, who can identify with victims of lynchings in a way that non-black students can't. Lecturers shouldn't lump a lesson on black liberation into an animal liberation lecture without considering what that juxtaposition feels like to someone black. Many BME students are already being made to feel that they are squeezing into spaces that weren't made for them. Lecture halls should not be one of those spaces.

The curricula of natural and clinical sciences have also failed to confront racism. Despite the focus on how race manifests in the social sciences, the essentialist notions of race that many of the natural and clinical sciences have traditionally adopted affects scientific research, and for medical students, it also affects how they go on to interact with their patients. Ayomide is a black medical student at Imperial College. The only

71

time that her cohort was taught how the black experience may be different from that of white patients was in discussions about sickle cell disease, and the fact that black people have an increased risk of high blood pressure. This gap in teaching is part of a trend of medical students being taught to look at race as anything other than a biologically-determined, epidemiological risk factor.

**Not once has anyone taught me how to approach my black patients outside of their disease, to approach them as a human, and that's something that I think medicine lacks in general.**
**–Ayomide**

This is a problem for two reasons: doctors may ignore that race is a lived experience which needs to be approached as a social factor; moreover, it reinforces the idea that race is a fixed, biological category. Addressing the role of racial categories is directly relevant to how doctors should interact with the diverse range of patients that they are going to encounter. We are doing future black patients a disservice by not educating doctors on what the black experience, and the black body, might mean for healthcare. Many black people are also more likely to get strokes, diabetes and heart disease. I'm not a medical student, and I won't pretend that I can intricately explain why that is the case – but it is, and our future doctors should be equipped to deal with that reality.

Academics such as Lundy Braun and Barry Saunders have extensively researched the ways in which medical students are still taught to 'correct' for race in a way that suggests that there are innate differences between races. These differences are more accurately described as social and environmental factors that have become genetically embedded in ancestral lines. For example, sickle cell disease and approaches to it have been racialised; it is viewed as a 'black disease', although the patterns of sickle cell incidence have more to do with the genetic evolutions of people who lived in malaria-endemic areas, because people with sickle cell are protected against malaria. While most people who fall into this category *are* black, it's not a black disease, and suggesting it is reinforces outdated notions of race as something innate and biological.

Legacies of scientific racism from the Enlightenment era, when black people were 'proven' to be three-fifths human, inherently different and incapable of acquiring 'higher faculties', still have implications for how the sciences are studied today. Race is not a biological category, it's a socially constructed one, and science curricula should respond to these changing ideas. Professors of science and medicine have as much of a duty as the academic staff in the social sciences to adapt their teaching and settings accordingly, introducing critical race theory to offset the racist assumptions that often permeate medical research.

Unfortunately, science is not value-neutral, and its research is affected by socio-political contexts which we know are racialised and gendered. The context affects the questions we ask in our research, the analytical categories we use, the perspectives we take and the assumptions we begin with. It also creates a problem for the things scientific research will miss – who it does not include, and the inevitable blind spots from the position of the researcher.

We must also question the origins of modern science as we know it. Too often, we are taught that science and technology are concepts that are *introduced* to non-Western societies. An idea such as that can be constructed as true only because we aren't ever taught where science really comes from. Our curriculum ignores the history of science at its inception, in which people of colour also played a monumental role. Chanda Prescod-Weinstein expands on this in her 'Decolonising Science Reading List', Akala spoke about it at the Oxford Union, and I'm glad that there appears to be a growing awareness of the fact that science also, in spite of its claims of 'objectivity', leaves much room to be diversified. Books, articles and videos on things like inclusive astronomy, black mathematicians and the feminist philosophy of physics are vital for deconstructing how we view science, its origins and the credibility of scientific contributions. Science and its curricula are not exempt from the critical reflexivity with which we should approach all our subject content.

The 'Liberating the Curriculum' working group at University College London (UCL) has partnered with the Medical School to explore what a diverse medical curriculum might look like. Dermatology, for example, is currently taught almost exclusively using images of how conditions manifest on white skin. 'It is generally far more difficult for myself and my medical student peers to identify a condition if you've never seen it on a darker skin colour before,' observe Gemma Wells and Maihma Lamba in a post on the project's website. The site has much more to say on being taught how symptoms may look different on black and brown bodies, the importance of ethnically diverse evidence bases, and being aware of factors to look out for in the test results of black patients.

However, alongside physical differences, medical students have to be educated on how a black person's relationship with mental health might differ from that of white people. Experiences of racism and discrimination have been linked to chronic conditions of stress by psychologist associations across the world. But according to a 2018 NHS report, black people are also four times more likely to be 'sectioned' than white people – that is, detained and treated against their will under the UK's mental health law. They are also more likely to be misdiagnosed with psychotic disorders and placed in secure wards. Moreover, there are cultural factors to be considered: for example, traditionally, many West African societies would ostracise people who suffered from mental illnesses. This can lead black people to be less forward with their doctors about any mental health challenges they're experiencing. Black people are also statistically more likely to be poorer, in many Western countries at least, and that comes with a range of associated stress-inducing factors.

**When you have a black patient, how do you approach that? This is a big thing in medicine that we don't do. The mental health aspect of a black person is a completely different thing from [that of] a white person. – Barbara**

University medical schools have a duty to prepare their students to treat *all* patients, including black patients, and their curriculum should reflect a willingness to do that. That almost a third of UK graduate doctors are BME is a statistic to be proud of – but the battle isn't won if their curriculum doesn't reflect that diversity too. (It is also relevant to add, however, that the BME category distorts this statistic in relation to black doctors, as it also includes a large proportion of Asian doctors.)

**The needs of my black patient are so different from the needs of my white patient because my white patient has not had to go through institutionalised racism or discrimination. – Ayomide**

Ayomide told me that after three years of medicine, she had learnt more about black mental health from the student-led ACS than she had from her medical degree. While we should be grateful that there are ACSs around the country that are making black mental health a priority, why should that be the job of black students, who have enough to deal with already?

*

While we wait on our curricula to catch up with us, most university courses offer the option to submit a dissertation, a long essay, or some other form of independent study. It's one aspect that can allow you to explore a topic in depth that your curriculum might not. This was something I looked forward to. At last, I thought: a space where I could finally write about whatever I wanted and take some ownership of my degree. I wanted to look at the role of international organisations like the World Bank in Nigeria's energy sector. I had become really interested in how Nigeria's grid and off-grid energy worked and how it was funded. I began research, reached out to experts in the area while I was in Nigeria, and set up interviews, but before all of that, I needed to find a supervisor. I went to see my Director of Studies, [the equivalent to an academic tutor] Duncan Kelly, who was always very supportive and entertained every single one of my rants about how hard it was to fit my African interests into the confines of my degree. I told him about my plans and he told me quite frankly, both to his regret and my disappointment, it would not be feasible. There was apparently no one in the entire politics department who specialised in anything even broadly West African. If I wanted to pursue a dissertation on this, I would have to change the angle to effectively make it less Nigerian. I met with a supervisor who said he could supervise me if I took Nigeria out of the equation, and another who said they had experience studying oil-producing states, but hadn't specifically studied any in West Africa.

I made the decision not to pursue it; it was made abundantly clear that I wouldn't be able to get the support that I needed. I managed to write, instead, two long essays for my African politics paper that I thoroughly enjoyed. But ultimately, I felt I had been limited by my own choices. Most of my peers had no issue finding supervisors for their interests in Schmitt and Marx and a whole bunch of other German political philosophers. But if you had interests in studying anything broadly West African, you would face issues.

A lot of black students had similar problems. Micha encountered difficulties when it was time to carry out her psychology research project:

> **Originally I really want[ed] to do something on race and potentially on implicit bias, and when I told my supervisor she was, like, 'I don't think there's anyone within PBS [psychological and behavioural studies] who could supervise you on that.' – Micha**

Some girls, like Arenike, push on with their plans despite the lack of support. Arenike ended up looking on Twitter for resources.

> **My dissertation was called formally, 'An Exploration of Racial Trauma in the Work of Solange Knowles, Claudia Rankine and Morgan Parker' . . . and that was basically a big 'fuck you' to the three years of my degree, where I hadn't been able to do anything political. [My dissertation was] not for an institution like Cambridge. It's speaking to black women and black non-binary people. That's who my target**

**audience was, but you know, there are no black academics in Cambridge, really, who could have looked at it. – Arenike.**

When our interests fall outside of what these institutions consider to be the norm, the onus is on us, the students, to sort ourselves out. The labour is outsourced to us because there's no one who is willing to explore our niches with us – especially given the scarcity of black academics. When it comes to topics that are centred around the black experience in particular, this is made even harder: you're probably going to have a white supervisor who has the privilege of being detached from the topic, and doesn't feel what you feel when you're working on it.

**My dissertation was on Caribbean identity formation, so essentially, how do Caribbean slaves operate under the scope of slavery in Jamaica . . . my supervisor was a white middle-aged guy. Lovely guy but distant from what I was researching. – Mikai**

You may even find that your white supervisor is afraid to criticise you, fearful that their position might be misconstrued. It's a hard balance to find. Given just how many academic staff reach professorial level without ever having to have these discussions about race, this is something you're very likely to encounter as a black student. And again, our academic experience suffers for it.

> **I'm learning as well . . . Just because I've chosen this topic and because it's personal to my identity, I'm not the expert on it and I expect to be given the same amount of conscientious critique as my peers – but by virtue of being a black woman writing about black women, I didn't. – Renée**

Another factor that influenced my decision on whether or not to do a dissertation was thinking about who would be grading it. Pursuing your 'adventurous' interests becomes a risk. You might find yourself writing about something that no one has studied in that depth before, and that is radical by virtue of its very existence. Renée wrote her dissertation on black transnational feminism:

> **As I predicted, one of my markers marked it ridiculously high and one of my markers marked it ridiculously low.**

One half of you wants to write fearlessly, but the other half of you is very scared, and justifiably so, that this might be marked by someone with little knowledge of your area of interest. Moreover, if your work involves any exploration of racism, you may be concerned that it will be scrutinised by someone who has never experienced racism or worse still, by someone who does not consider racism worthy of academic critique.

You can't write unapologetically and with confidence about blackness and hope that your paper blends into the background. It's going to stand out. It's hard to predict whether that will work in your favour because chances are, not many people have done it before. If you find yourself considering writing a dissertation on black issues, do it because you will produce something that you're proud of, not because you think it will get a high grade. It might not. And although quite a few of us ended up disappointed, and feeling that our labour hadn't attracted the reward it deserved, we produced pieces that we're still proud of. That feeling lasts much longer.

## Peers and Professors

It's not just the reading lists that may make you feel isolated at university. Your lectures, the people in them and the people delivering them play a key role in your academic experience, and can serve as another reminder of your minority status in this space.

I had an accident with plantain five days before freshers' week, and I was in hospital when I should have been in my first few lectures (in hindsight, this is quite a funny story, but I will bore you with it later). When I finally went to my first lecture, I was on a mission to find anyone and everyone black. It actually wasn't that bad – there were a few of us. I sat in front of Courtney, who I had met at a careers event a few weeks earlier. I wanted to lock in that black girl solidarity nice and early because I knew I was going to need it.

Lectures are central to your academic experience of university. In the day-to-day of lectures and essays, I came to realise that for the most part, HSPS was anomalous in the relative diversity not just of its curriculum but also of its students. For most people, the unequal representations in their curricula were replicated in the student makeup.

**I've never seen a black British person do engineering in my school. – Adaobi**

Adaobi went to Manchester. Chelsea was the only black girl in her history lectures. Nathania is one of two. Mikai was one of three.

Diversity in lectures and seminars isn't just about who you sit with, and how you make friends. For most of the time, as a black student you're largely invisible within the curriculum. Going back to my very questionable industrialisation lecture that completely left out the role of slavery, my worries were compounded by the fact that I was surrounded by largely non-black people who couldn't see what was wrong with it.

**I went to a lecture on gender which was part of HAP [historical argument and practice] and the lecturer only spoke about white men and white women. I remember leaving that lecture and I was so angry. I did not go to another HAP lecture after that. – Chelsea**

We could be sitting right under a lecturer's nose, and yet he or she would still manage to look over us, over our blackness and over our histories. It's one thing to be constantly isolated by your lecture content, but having to deal with that alone, in silence, stings more.

You feel invisible when you're left off the syllabus, but the moment a topic slightly related to black people comes up in a lecture, you are suddenly hypervisible. You're just as much a subject of intrigue as the black person on the PowerPoint slide. You are now seen, but not in a way over which you have any control. Meanwhile, the white students around you are doing mental gymnastics trying to project the story of this black subject of your lecture onto you. They are learning something that's going to mediate how they see and experience other black people, and you, being one of the only black people in your lecture, are their first victim, the unelected and unwilling representative of the whole black population.

This might be uncomfortable. Discussing anything mildly black-ish can lead people to assume that you are well-versed on the topic simply because it includes people with the same colour skin as you. Sometimes, you might actually be knowledgeable about the topic, or have experiences that mean that you can speak with some kind of authority. But equally, your opinion on it may be held in an exceptionally high esteem that you haven't really earned. You're no expert – you're there to learn too. Don't turn around and stare at me when the lecturer starts talking about the Rwandan genocide because I know as little as you do.

That's one way it might go. Some budding racists might think that now is a great time to argue with you, shrouding their prejudices in so much academic jargon that you almost think they've said something of value. Colonialism is a common one. I would be very surprised if you got through a lecture on colonialism without someone suggesting that actually colonialism was great, and implying that there is something inherently wrong with the millions of victims of empire.

**In this seminar, one boy piped up ... 'But at what point do we think Africans will take responsibility and stop blaming neocolonialism for everything?' – Chelsea.**

There are always going to be provocative students. But the point is that their questionable views are validated and given weight in these environments, especially in instances when the lecturer lets it slide. Fope had it in their political geography module:

**One person in class was like, 'You know what? Colonialism wasn't that bad; they gave us trains, you know.' For the rest of the lecture, I just felt like [I had] indigestion, because it pissed me off ... [The lecturer] was just like, 'That's an interesting perspective. Let's move on.' I could tell he probably was really uncomfortable with**

**what the guy said, but if you have privilege, call it out. And the fact that he didn't really frustrated me.**

In seminars or other forms of small-group teaching that thrive on student interaction, a lot of black girls would retreat. We would hold our points back because we didn't want to come across as loud or angry, thereby living up to the tropes that society repeatedly projects onto us. You also don't want be accused of 'playing the race card', and as the Imposter syndrome begins to kick in again, you find yourself retreating.

**When these things happen again and again, you just check out. And I think for a long time in Cambridge, that's what I did. – Arenike**

**I would almost make an effort *not* to contribute.\* – Eireann**

**I don't want people to view me as angry. I don't want people to view me as too loud. I don't want people to think I'm always making it about race. But also . . . I didn't want to come across as stupid and let down my fellow black women . . . carrying that on your shoulders at eighteen**

\* Emphasis added.

**when you're trying to get your degree is quite a lot to put on yourself. – Courtney**

Black representation figures are even worse when it comes to teaching staff. Data released by the Higher Education Statistics Agency in 2017 shows that British universities employ more black staff as cleaners, porters and receptionists than they do as lecturers and professors. In my three years at Cambridge, I had only *one* black lecturer, a Mexican woman named Mónica Figueroa, who was in charge of my sociology of race paper. I knew of only *one* black supervisor in African politics – Njoki Wamai. I had heard of another black faculty member, Malachi McIntosh, but he left before I could meet him. He once posted a tweet that compared his time at Cambridge to the 2017 horror film *Get Out*\* – hardly a compliment. Given how hard it can be to be a black student at Cambridge, I can only imagine what that experience might be like as a member of staff. When I heard that he had left, I was hardly surprised.

**Why would you want to work somewhere where you don't feel comfortable? Because I wanted to leave Cambridge after a week. – Kenya**

---

\* If you are unfamiliar with Jordan Peele's film, among many other themes it explores different levels of racism, from the subtle sort veiled in liberal ignorance to the more overtly violent kind.

A shockingly small 1.8 per cent of all academic staff in the UK are black, according to Advance HE, an independent organisation focused on research in higher education. We represent a lower proportion than any other ethnic group; Asian staff make up 6 per cent and white staff almost 90 per cent. The proportion of black staff shrinks further, to 1.4 per cent, if we look only at those who are British. It shrinks further still if we look at those who are at professorial level – to 0.6 per cent. Considering just black women takes us down to 0.13 per cent – of almost 19,000 professors in the UK, only twenty-five are black women. Most of the people we interviewed for this book had not been taught by anyone black at all during their whole degree.

**Patricia Daley, the one that we call on every single Black History Month to come and give her thoughts, she's the only black female faculty staff that I know of. – Renée**

**I don't know if it's that [fewer] black people are becoming professors or [fewer] black people are being employed as professors even when they're qualified. Whichever one it is, they're both problems. – Ayomide**

I refuse to believe that this is because there are no black academics who are qualified – because the truth is, there are. But these numbers are largely a result of a cycle of underrepresentation. For as long as we continue to see academic spaces as places that black people cannot penetrate and cannot excel in, we perpetuate the cycle of self-exclusion. The ivory tower of academia is still pretty ivory, and it is evidenced in our curricula, our reading lists and our lecture content. Before they've climbed high enough to be able to penetrate the system, a lot of black academics find they have had enough of the structural and systemic racism in the field – and frankly, I don't blame them.

For the few who find ways to stick around, we are grateful. Having black, or even broadly BME, supervisors and lecturers is refreshing. They get it. They don't think your black examples are 'adventurous'; they understand why they're necessary. They encourage the use of these examples, and appreciate their importance in a way that not all white supervisors do. Micha wrote a sociology essay on black hair for her black supervisor, Tanisha Spratt:

> **Firstly, I get to study this? But secondly, I think even if I wrote about this for a white supervisor, they might be like, 'What are you talking about?' It's so cool that she just gets it. – Micha**

For once, we are relieved of the burden of having to teach our own supervisors what it means to be black.

**There was a time when I genuinely thought I wanted to go into academia, and I still kind of do – but I've not seen black professors. I have never even had a black school teacher before. - Ayomide**

When Ayomide said this, it really upset me, because academia needs more people like her – it needs more people like us. This is how underrepresentation reproduces itself. I'm lucky enough to have my dad, whose academic career reminds me that this is something within my reach, but I also recognise that this is an uncommon privilege. We should never, as black girls, feel limited by the lack of black academics we are likely to encounter at university. If we ever feel called upon to go into academia, I hope that we will find people who can support us along the way, and believe that we can be just as qualified as any, anywhere: be the Monicas and the Malachis and the Tanishas that we so need. They remind us that we *can*, even when the numbers are ranged against us.

For as long as the people making decisions on what to include and what not to include in our reading lists are largely old, white men who don't understand what it feels like for us to encounter Eurocentric curricula, it will be difficult to create change. While I'm sure that the minority of black staff are doing their best to make change from within, their underrepresentation is helpful context for understanding why many of the efforts to liberate our curricula are coming from student-led movements.

## #DecolonisetheCurriculum

We have a right, as black students, to have our stories accurately and completely represented in our curricula. To take ownership over our degrees requires us to show our senior faculty staff what it is that they may not be able to see from their ivory towers. 'Decolonise the Curriculum', 'Why is My Curriculum White', and 'Liberate My Degree' are some of the student-led movements working to make these changes, made up of students across the country, and the world, trying to make sure that their negative experiences with their curricula are not reproduced.

The impact of the #DecolonisetheCurriculum movement has varied by university. We welcomed the announcement in 2017 that Oxford University had made it compulsory for history undergraduates to take a non-European paper, in response to the Why is My Curriculum White? movement. Departments across Cambridge also put together working groups that held almost-weekly open forums and events, in which students could highlight issues with curricula, propose solutions and alternatives, and draft letters for the consideration of senior faculty staff. The work of the 'Decolonise English' group culminated in an open letter addressed to the university's English faculty.

**We believe that for the English department to truly boast academically rigorous thought and practice, non-white authors and postcolonial thought must be incorporated meaningfully into the curriculum. This is not a call for the exclusion of white men from reading lists, needless to say: it is a call to re-centre the lives of other marginalized writers who have been silenced by the canon. It is a call to not be arrogant enough to assume civilization began with the writing of white men.**

Over 150 people signed the letter, which also included a list of practical suggestions that the faculty could incorporate in order to diversify their curriculum, including diversity training for supervisors and making the postcolonial and related literatures paper a mandatory requirement for first year students.

The 'Decolonise HSPS' group has been working with the HSPS faculty for years on specific modifications to the reading lists. The extent of the changes to the first-year politics paper in the past three years is a testament to their hard work. Frantz Fanon, for example, is no longer included as an add-on in a lecture on violence, but is studied as a theorist in his own right.

The working group drew up an 'Alternative Reading List', which was shared widely online. It opens with a lengthy introduction outlining its goals, beginning:

> **In the context of academic learning, decolonization may be understood as the intellectually rigorous and honest acknowledgement and recognition of the histories of violence that underlie present systems of power and knowledge. Among its key aims is a disentanglement from, and decentring of, hegemonic epistemologies and ways of knowing.**

The twenty-eight-page document was the work of students, many of whom were in their final year and drowning in exam revision, but who gave up their time regardless. Featured on the curriculum are books on racism in the Enlightenment, literature on the Cold War from the perspectives of countries in the global south, and broader critical race theory. The resource has received an incredible response. Lucy Mayblin, a senior lecturer at Sheffield University (ranked second in the country for sociology), has included the resource in an online 'global social theory' reading list. The online resource pool is available for staff everywhere seeking to decolonise their departments' curricula and for the students seeking to do the decolonising that the departments may not be.

The thing with these movements is that they work. Thanks to student efforts, and to the staff who are open to supporting them, there are some exemplary, less white curricula out there that are leading the pack. Sociology at Cambridge was refreshing. I got to write essays about race and gender and intersectionality, and my experiences didn't feel as marginalised as they had for so long. In my final year, even though I had specialised in politics and international relations, I took a sociology of race paper. In my final exams, I wrote an essay in which I explored the power dynamics perpetuated by black natural hair YouTubers. I felt I could bring my full self to every supervision and every assignment. This was the one paper where I felt that my experiences were welcomed and encouraged.

When Mikai spoke about the English degree at Warwick, I was shocked to learn that English wasn't as canonical everywhere, and that some university departments had an awareness and appreciation for books other than Homer's:

**My English degree differed to a lot of people's – that's why I'm glad I ended up at Warwick. [On our reading lists,] we had Assata [Shakur]'s autobiography, we had a lot of South American women writers. We had quite a few black writers, black women writers.**

In the same paper at Warwick for which you can study Homer's *Iliad* – seen as an iconic, canonical part of ancient Greek literature – you can also study Ngugi wa Thiong'o's *Petals of Blood*. This piece of social and political criticism of Kenya's post-colonial context, written in the form of an allegorical crime story, was so radical for its time that wa Thiong'o was arrested in the months after its publication. Rarely do I encounter curricula that acknowledge that writers such as Homer and wa Thiong'o belong in the same category of greatness – so rarely, that I am in disbelief each time I do.

For curricula that aren't quite there yet, we as students can work to decolonise our own academic pathways. In my international relations essays, I would introduce examples of how the United Nations has been complicit in propagating neocolonialism under the guise of African 'development' narratives, and discuss how the role of the United States in sponsoring tyrannical dictators should disqualify them from being able to call themselves anything near liberal. I would write about the Cold War, but also discuss what the precarious political situation meant for African political leaders. This was my personal battle of resistance. I didn't have it in me to fight the whole system, but I did what I could from the confines of my own desk. I didn't give World War I *or* II any more time than the minimum I had to. Without question, World War I and II were monumental events in history, and their outcomes have shaped the ideological climate that has since persisted. However, it's not all the history that there is.

Offering diverse curricula is not always easy. Sometimes I would find that faculties had attempted to 'diversify' by introducing ideas from postcolonial contexts that did not easily fit. In order to study these topics, it often felt as if the onus was on us, as the few BME students, to create tenuous links between white and non-white contexts when they weren't always obvious, or even there at all. In my third year, for example, I had the opportunity to study patriotism, nationalism and postcolonialism – or at least, so it seemed. In reality, it was an attempt to throw Frantz Fanon and Aimé Césaire into a lecture on liberal and republican nationalism. (If you have no clue what any of those words mean: it's hard, made deliberately so, and there's a very limited amount of available literature to guide you.)

While many of my white colleagues could choose to answer another question or do another essay, I felt compelled to answer anything that allowed me to engage with the black authors that were so few and far between on our syllabuses. If I spent so much time complaining that they weren't present enough, then surely I had to take full advantage of the rare occasions in which they were? I felt I had an obligation to do black theorists and writers justice, even as they were forcefully squeezed in as 'add-ons' to a curriculum that is still very white. And it was another instance in which I was alienated from my peers, who didn't share this sense of duty and obligation, and felt that they had true freedom in the paper choices that they made. We're fighting for curricula that allow us to also study black people in their own rights, not just as add-ons to tick a 'diversity' box.

The key point here is to speak out. If you find yourself in a position in which you can be heard, let your lecturers and your supervisors know that they will get more out of you if your curriculum is inclusive, and also reflects your reality. I would give my supervisors recommendations and ask them why we were not exploring the fact that all but one of the countries tried by the International Criminal Court have been African. There are, after all, war criminals to be found in places other than African countries who haven't been brought to justice in this way. I would ask my supervisors why we studied governments from a perspective that assumed that Western liberal democracy is the only formula for good governance. I challenged my curriculum because I felt that the movement started with me.

Arenike tried to speak up too:

**I was like, 'Why haven't we studied anyone who's not white?' And he was like, 'Oh yeah, I don't know, I don't really like, read those things' – bla**

**bla bla. I'm just looking at him like, 'Wow. You're a PhD student. How have you gotten to where you are without reading these texts? How? How am I, an undergrad, smarter than you?'**

**That's when I knew university was a scam.
– Arenike**

You may also find supervisors who are willing to listen to your complaints. They may not always know exactly how to help, but they want to learn. My Director of Studies would always ask for suggestions; where he couldn't help me explore particular interests, he would direct me to the people and literature that could. I had a supervisor, Ali Meghji, who would send me articles and texts that weren't on my reading lists but which enabled me to develop those interests that weren't given space on my curriculum.

**My Director of Studies, Deborah [Thom], she was really nice. I remember one day I said 'misogynoir'* and she was like, 'What's that? I've never heard of that. Explain it to me.' You'd have**

---

* Misogynoir is a term used to describe misogyny, i.e. prejudice against women, that is specifically directed at black women. The term attributed to the American queer black feminist Moya Bailey who used it to discuss the way race and gender oppression co-exist specifically in pop culture.

**to explain a lot of things to her, but what I liked was she was willing to listen. – Courtney**

It's hard to say what a decolonised curriculum might look like. While some who would ask that question are often seeking to belittle the movement and the need for it, it is still worth asking. Are we trying to study the world in terms of what it might have looked like in a pre-colonial context? Because if that's the case, how do we access non-written histories, or histories in dead languages, or oral histories that have been lost and transformed through generations? If it's clear how much of our very existences, and the ideas that we have developed while existing, are products of colonialism, then what room is there for us in a decolonised curriculum? To truly 'decolonise' our curriculum requires a radical overthrow of what we even consider knowledge and how it is produced.

**We assume decolonising the curriculum is just adding a few more black writers or Asian writers or whoever. I think to truly decolonise might mean a different system all together, and I don't know what that looks like. – Eireann**

The same question should be asked of the way we use the word 'intersectional'. The term was coined by Kimberlé Crenshaw, and sets out an analytical framework for us to understand that the different axes of our identity cannot be considered in isolation. It was developed specifically in reference to black women, whose dual burdens of racism and sexism interact to create a unique experience of oppression. More broadly, it is now used to refer to how we approach 'diversity' for those whose layers of oppression are compounded. But what does a truly intersectional approach to a topic really look like? Chanda Prescod-Weinstein writes:

**Theorizing about what an intersectional perspective does to our discourse and remembering that Black women exist are simply not the same thing. The former requires effort, and the latter should be your baseline.**

It requires us to go beyond merely acknowledging that black women and their histories are worthy of study, and beyond including them merely to meet an arbitrary requirement.

As black women who have experienced all of the above, we should rally round any efforts made by different groups or movements to promote a more diversified curriculum in all the different disciplines. The work that such groups do is extremely necessary for a future in which black girls aren't shocked to find themselves on curricula, and can truly identify with the authors they're made to read.

## The Black Attainment Gap

The whiteness of academia is ruining our experience of university. It isolates any non-white interests that we may have before we arrive, it establishes an environment that is not conducive for us to pursue those interests, it affects the subjects that we choose to study and the industries that we are able to penetrate, and it dissuades many of us from staying the course of academia until we are in positions high enough to fix the issues ourselves.

Fundamentally, for as long as academia stays this white, black students will continue to fall short. If everything I have said so far isn't enough to show that, the 24 per cent attainment gap between black and white students should be. According to a 2018 report by Advance HE, 79.6 per cent of white UK undergraduates achieved a first or a 2:1 – but the number drops 24 percentage points to 55.5 per cent for black UK students. I know that this isn't because we aren't capable. It is because several factors – among them lopsided curricula, the lack of black academics and the difficulty finding support in navigating these institutions – are holding us back from reaching our full potential. If not properly handled, the impact these structures uniquely have on us can persist long after we graduate.

Changing these statistics is going to involve more than just black students working hard. Academic staff, from those charged with setting and teaching the national curriculum, to those at universities who have autonomy in drawing up reading lists, must listen to students and work alongside them for the betterment of our academic experience. Even though the odds are stacked against us as black students, I hope that others find strength in knowing that we have all been there, and that we've got firsts and 2:1s in spite of these odds – and that we can begin to change these statistics.

## 3

## *Mental Health*

Chelsea

One morning at the beginning of my second year at university, I bounced out of bed and knocked on my best friend Holly's door. She lived next to me on our tiny narrow corridor at college, and I patiently waited for her to open up so that we could align our schedules for the day. Within seconds of her letting me in, the contraband coffee machine on her desk was already sputtering out two espresso shots. I was in love with this coffee machine and had become mildly obsessed with my morning coffee hit. *It even frothed milk* . . . If I'm honest, I was sure it wouldn't be long before we owned T-shirts saying, 'Don't talk to me until I've had my coffee!' or 'Rise and Grind!' Drinking coffee at university signified peak adulting and sophistication, not to mention endless social opportunities to meet friends in really expensive cafés. (Not that I did that any more.)

I gulped down the espresso, said goodbye to Holly and went back to my room to study. My room was my sanctuary. Sitting at my desk, lost in work, allowed me to temporarily escape the pressure bubble of Cambridge life. And it wasn't as if I really needed to leave: the canteen and college café were downstairs; my supervisions were upstairs, and the launderette was down the corridor. My room was where I was the most productive, unlike most of my fellow students, who had set up a shifting camp in the twenty-four-hour library, armed with their own cardboard cups of coffee, modafinil and rollies for the rare cigarette break.

As you can imagine, however, staying in my room didn't create the most outgoing of lifestyles. By that morning, I had missed around three weeks of lectures. I hadn't even left the college in nine days. The strange thing was, no one batted an eyelid. It was so easy to slip under the radar. We were all working, and we all had our own deadlines to meet. It wasn't weird that the corridors were silent throughout the day. It wasn't weird if you hadn't seen someone in a few days.

Back at my desk, it didn't take long for the caffeine to hit me. But this time, rather than feeling energised, I felt jittery. I was finding it increasingly hard to concentrate, and became very conscious that I was alone from the familiar silence in the halls. I headed downstairs to the café to fill up my water bottle and buy a sandwich. As I went to pay, I was offered a free latte by one of the staff members. Really, I should have declined but the student in me popped out. A *free* coffee? Unheard of. It also had a smiley face carefully stencilled on top of the frothed milk. How could I say no?

But I should have done. Twenty minutes later, I was experiencing one of the worst anxiety attacks that I have ever had in my life. It was debilitating. For around six hours I stayed in my room alone – not out of choice, but because I couldn't move. I sat at my desk shaking profusely, still trying to push through my weekly task of reading seven articles and completing a 2,500-word essay. Wave after wave of panic hit me. My heart was beating so hard I feared that I was likely to drop down dead any minute, and no one would find me until it was too late. Death by coffee.

How would I explain to someone that this crisis was triggered by coffee? Everyone drinks coffee, every day! It felt ridiculous. But perhaps most worrying was that I didn't even know who to go to in the first place. Was it my own belief that this crisis wasn't *serious enough*? Or was it that I still wasn't ready to admit that my anxiety had reached a worrying level? Over the past few years, it had become increasingly bad: stress-induced panic attacks, overthinking and bouts of self-doubt. I had absorbed it as part of my personality, thinking that it was just another character trait.

Eventually, I built up the courage to text a friend and ask if I could sit in her room. Luckily, she was in and we sat down on her bed and watched season 10 of *Ru Paul's Drag Race*, my heart still thumping worryingly fast. I cursed the coffee gods, and made a promise to never put myself in that position again.

## Black Effect: Mental Health at University

Universities across the country are currently in the grip of a mental health crisis. In 2015–16, over 15,000 first-year students (UK-based) disclosed mental health issues. Yet a Freedom of Information request by the Liberal Democrat Norman Lamb revealed that at 100 universities, students had to wait up to four months to access counselling and mental health support. Suicide rates among university students in England and Wales have risen to seriously concerning levels, with ninety-five students committing suicide between 2016 and 2017 – one every four days. At the University of Bristol alone, there were ten suicides in the space of eighteen months.

This comes at a time when conversations regarding mental health are opening up. Society, it seems, is beginning to realise that mental health is important. And nowhere is the question of mental health more important than at university. Most people with a mental illness first develop symptoms between the ages of sixteen and twenty-five.

**By third year if I met someone who hadn't experienced a mental health problem, I thought that that was more notable than meeting someone who had. – Micha**

Each university has been left to its own devices to decide how best to tackle mental health issues within their own student populations. The University of Cumbria, for example, made suicide prevention and awareness training available for all staff in a bid to create 'compassionate campuses'. Over 12 per cent of all staff have now been trained. Similarly, the University of Brunel's security officers have been trained by the disability and counselling services to adequately respond to mental health crises among students.

There are, however, significant variations in provision surrounding mental health care within UK universities, with some universities doing much more than others. This signifies the varying ideas of what mental health actually is, and when it warrants external attention. As a result, some universities experience dramatic increases in demand. With the breaking down of the stigma of mental health and disabilities, it is clear that more students are starting to come forward and seek help. It's one thing to acknowledge that a university is addressing mental health – but just how well are they really doing it?

Some might say that the university environment and culture thrive on self-inflicted suffering. In my case, it was promising myself that I would eat breakfast only *after* I finished the chapter that I had failed to finish the night before; promising myself that I would sleep only *after* I finished everything on my to-do list for that day. For the first few weeks of university, it was all about keeping up, and that meant spending hours in the college library. This lifestyle was continuously validated every time I logged into Instagram to see the obligatory 3-a.m.-in-the-library-and-I-haven't-slept-in-forty-eight-hours photo of other students. It was a constant reminder that if I thought that I was working hard, there was always someone working harder. But by the end of a week-long stint in the library, I was snapped fast asleep on the library desk with my laptop next to me. Clearly, I just couldn't keep up.

At university, I experienced some of the worst mental health issues I have ever faced. I'm still unsure whether these issues developed as a result of university, or whether the transition process unearthed pre-existing conditions. In my first year, I remember being totally overwhelmed by Cambridge's email system. I hadn't really used email before university, believe it or not (my princesskwakye@hotmail.com account was exclusively for MSN Messenger). When I received an email from my supervisor asking what date and time I'd like to meet, I would draft a response. Then re-draft. Then delete it all and start again. Then re-draft. Then Google 'how do you sign off an email when you don't know the person?' Then call a friend to check what they had sent to their supervisor. Then ask them to read my attempt.

Only *then* would it be safe to send. I also spent an unnecessary amount of time worrying about cycling. My route to lectures became an imagined race course that would, I was certain, result in death-by-car at any moment. I returned to Cambridge after my first term with an extreme sports helmet clamped on my head . . . you know, just in case. My point is, the way I learnt to understand my own mental health was unexpected. There wasn't a 'sudden' change.

But something was going on – for me, and for others like me. And like many people, I didn't have a clue who was the best person to go to when I felt that I needed to talk. As expected, the added stresses associated with transitioning into a new environment definitely had an impact, as well as moving away from home, loneliness, deadlines, finances and getting to grips with this thing called 'email'.

*

There is already substantial evidence to suggest that racial discrimination and marginalisation contribute to mental illnesses within young black people in the UK. The 2014 Adult Psychiatric Morbidity Survey (APMS) discovered that the prevalence of common mental health problems varied dramatically by ethnic group for women, but not for men. Black British and non-British women were both found to be more likely to have a 'common mental health problem' (29.3 per cent) by comparison with white British women (20.9 per cent).

Black women are seen as the epitome of self-sacrifice, holding it down for everyone around them and always considering themselves last – a glamorised stereotype. Simultaneously, the 'strong black woman' is also policed to make sure she doesn't come across as *too* strong. We all know that we can't possibly be the *angry* one or the *loud* one. In fact, we're constantly told to hold it all in – the emotion (and/or rage). There is no licence to show emotion that allows us to be vulnerable, especially when many of our mental health issues are rooted in daily experiences of racism.

**I don't want to be strong all the time. And it's not even a strength in myself, I have to be strong for my people, strong for my community, strong in relationships. The black woman always has to be the strong one and that's a silencing mechanism because it means we're not able to express weakness, we're not allowed to express vulnerability, and I think that's a fundamental flaw in our conceptions of black women. – Renée**

How such tropes play out in university environments is rarely spoken about. In December 2018, the *Guardian* began its 'Racial Bias' series, which aimed to document racial inequalities within the UK. If you're a person of colour in Britain, I'm sure its report didn't come as a shock. In fact, I pretty much scrolled past it. It revealed that black students in England are 1.5 times more likely to drop out than their white and Asian counterparts.

The uncomfortable truth is that universities in the UK are hotbeds for explicit and implicit racism. From the words 'MONKEY' and 'NIGGA' found written on Warwick student Faramade Ifaturoti's bunch of bananas to fellow students chanting 'we hate the blacks' outside Rufaro Chisango's room at Nottingham Trent University, issues such as these are *not* isolated. On my first day at Cambridge, I was asked whether I could dance because 'black people are really good at dancing' – as if I was a minstrel ready to spring into action at the clap of a hand. For anyone still wondering: no, I can't dance. Not all black people can. Thank you for coming to my TED Talk.

**On my first day, someone asked me if I was in a gang – Kenya**

**We had a post office on campus. The post office guy said, 'Oh, do you work here?' . . . I get that a lot on campus, 'Do you work here?' or 'Excuse me, could you show me where this is?' Am I a sales assistant of Warwick? – Mikai**

The problem is not limited to overt instances of racism. Racial microaggressions are commonplace for most black girls at universities. The term 'microaggressions' was coined by Harvard professor Chester M. Pierce in 1970 to describe the insults and dismissals he witnessed non-black Americans inflicting on African Americans. Since then, the term has been revised to include commonplace and daily exchanges – not being acknowledged, or complimenting good use of English. For me, what was most tiresome was having to always consider whether something was a microaggression or not. Imagine going through your day-to-day life and having to wonder whether someone has treated you differently because you're black – because more often than not, the answer is yes.

The majority of the UK's top universities are rife with environmental microaggressions. In the not-too-distant past, a lot of people actively didn't want you here. The remnants of those beliefs are still very much apparent and play an active part in our daily university experiences, from the portraits of white, heterosexual, upper-class men on the walls to still being the only black student in a year group.

**You want to talk about other political and structural reasons why your mental health can be severely affected. But when you bring those**

**things up, it's like, 'Oh, you're making it polit-
ical. . .' And there's often a failure to acknowledge
that they're really intertwined. – Micha**

Understanding of mental health cannot be detached
from daily racial experiences, which in turn means that
the mental health of black women is largely political.
Racial microaggressions are subtle yet significant forms
of racism that may seem harmless, but their cumulative
and constant burden can lead to a dramatic impact on
mental wellbeing. Sadly, many fail to recognise or
acknowledge this fundamental fact, because to them if
it can't quantified or measured, it doesn't exist.

## Black Excellence?

As a black girl, you are subject to a number of expectations: the expectation to be strong, for example – but also, if you manage to get into university, and especially one of the top universities in the country, the expectation to excel. For those unfamiliar with it: the term 'Black Excellence' can be used to commend or congratulate someone black for achieving a certain goal. Alternatively, it can be used in a communal sense, as a means of furthering a positive perception of black people. Think Diddy's Instagram captions: 'It's bigger than being billionaires, it's about owning our culture and leading the revolution #blackexcellence' or simply, 'B L A C K E X C E L L E N C E'. Black Excellence characterises everything that mainstream media has taught us *not* to believe. It draws on a golden thread running throughout the black community, stirring up a sense of pride and inspiration around anyone who succeeds in generating a positive perception.

At Bath Spa University, a photo exhibition entitled 'Black Excellence' displayed the faces of what they called 'the incredible array of BME talent' at the university. Staff, students and alumni were all included as a way of bringing attention to why Black History Month is so important and why it should continue to be celebrated. One of the subjects was Dr Olivette Otele, the first black, female history professor in the UK. Representation has to start somewhere, and from my own social echo chamber, black excellence narratives highlight the beauty in black people sharing a moment together. Yet some of our understandings of black excellence still revolve around white validation. It's hard to define, by our own standards, what it means to be successful. It becomes a form of respectability politics, whereby only a certain *type* of black student or person can be 'successful'. There is an extra shout-out or an even louder toot for a young black person who gains a place at Oxford or Cambridge. Taking up space in traditionally white institutions is heralded as the epitome of resistance – in reality, it's more likely to be acquiescence, accommodation and compromise. Black people (in this case black students) subsequently feel the pressure to live up to unrealistic expectations of self. This pressure all too often impacts our mental health.

All of a sudden, your actions and very existence become the blueprint for all things black. For me, that meant not showing my tutors, lecturers and support staff any signs of my anxiety, because I wanted to prove to people that Cambridge wasn't *too* hard for me and that *I* didn't struggle. Throughout my degree, I tried to demonstrate that I wasn't 'just' a black student that they had let in as part of some access ploy, that I was as good as everyone else.

Simply existing in white spaces can be exhausting – so you can only imagine the pressure of the added cloud of Black Excellence hanging over your every move. Excellence doesn't give you the opportunity to fail and disappoint, nor the room for trial and error. Ọrẹ admitted that from the outset many may have viewed her as an example of Black Excellence. As a Cambridge student and chair of one of the most successful ACSs in the UK, she has continued to push a positive perception of black students, and was vocal about what else needed to be done to ensure that black students are fully included at traditionally white universities. But often the reality was that:

**Everyone is watching you. The eyes are on you. Don't just be the black person who got in . . . be the black person who got in and got a first. The black person who got in, got a first and got a training contract. Got in, got a first, and got five training contracts!**

Black Excellence pressure does not stop when you accept your university place. The narrative means that many black students are automatically expected to stand for the whole black community. Mikai spoke about how this understanding of acceptability is a constant cycle:

> **I think that black students always have to be proving something to someone, which is very damaging. If you're not proving to your parents, you're proving to your tutor, you're proving to your examiner, proving to somebody that what you stand for is worth it, is worth attention, is worth glory.**

Most of this behavioural pattern is engendered by a feeling of 'gratitude' experienced by most black students. There's a belief that you've been given a *chance*. You can't be the one to mess it up. But what happens if you are struggling? Or think that you are messing up? The 24 per cent black attainment gap at university reveals a downward spiral: it is clear that there is a faltering point (or phase) between black students entering university on a par with other students, and yet leaving with lower grades.

If I'm honest, I'm still conflicted around the Black Excellence narrative. I found it destructive at times, and used it as an excuse to push myself to impossible heights. At other times, I saw how far the narrative encouraged students to fulfil their existing potential, knowing that there is a whole community rooting for them. Either way, as long as success is defined on your own terms and beliefs, I give you permission to write your own Diddy Instagram captions.

## Getting Help

One weekend in between exams, I decided to go home. I sat quietly in the kitchen and watched my mum wash plates in the sink. She could tell that I was tired. I had huge bags under my eyes and had fallen asleep at least two times that day. After five minutes of silence, she turned to face me and said, 'I'm proud of you no matter what. The end grade doesn't matter as long as you try your best, you've done enough.' I can't explain how perfectly timed those words were. My philosophy as the youngest child had always been, 'Chelsea, you need to work hard and sort yourself out, so your parents can go back to Ghana. They can't be worrying about you.' I wanted to, and still plan to, look after my parents. But with that comes a heightened level of stress, commitment and pressure.

For many students, it's easy to imagine families or support systems as sponges, ready to absorb our traumas and problems, helping us to feel better. But for many black families, 'strong' is valued, and persistence and resilience are favoured. The cultural understanding of mental health is different, and so is the language to conceptualise it, meaning that when mental health problems appear, African and Caribbean parents can be slow to respond. Parents or relatives may start to blame themselves and ask what they have done to 'fail' you. Some parents might tell you to pray and strengthen your relationship with God. Many parents or carers may wonder what you have to complain about: you should be *grateful*. Most of our parents came from places where mental health problems were hardly spoken of, to the point that they were made invisible. Yet here we are: educated, likely to become employable, the world at our feet, pretty much – but we *still* have something to moan about.

**When I was younger a family friend said, 'Oh, anorexia is a white person's disease.' So, it just feels like if you are suffering from a mental health issue, then you're being weak or you're too Westernised. I think definitely now, at least amongst my parents' generation, the kids are getting more literate in the language of mental health. It's getting better. – Arenike**

African and Caribbean communities in the UK deal with mental health problems differently to white British society. The relationship between mental health provision in the UK and the black community is complex. For starters, black men and women are more likely to engage with mental health services through the courts or the police than on their own terms.

**I've always thought that with being Caribbean, a lot comes from legacies of slavery. The idea about having been through so much historical trauma, probably as a collective . . . you haven't had a chance or time to be vulnerable, to be weak, because you have to just keep pushing on. Especially if [you're] living in the UK and enduring racism. – Micha**

**You can't expect them [African parents] to be perfect when nobody has paid them any attention, no one has even told them that you're allowed to feel these emotions, they don't even have the room to be upset. My parents actually knew I was depressed before I knew. – Adaobi**

The link between mental illness and racial trauma is something that most black people are very familiar with. Conversations surrounding mental health tend to skirt over the various elements that explain the position of black people today. The system's inability to work with socio-political forces that disproportionately affect black people renders our unique experiences invisible. Despite being less likely to receive the support we need and facing isolation within wider society, we're yet to consider how black people would benefit from a wholly inclusive service. It's time we stepped away from the assumption that mental health is apolitical.

Students are starting to seek professional support such as counselling a lot earlier, rather than having to do so when reaching crisis point. Upon reaching an agreement with yourself that help is needed, counselling can be a good way to air existing issues or past traumas. However, many black students, particularly black women, may find that counselling at university is not always the best option when dealing with mental health problems – most of which originate and continue to exist because of issues to do with race. The ease with which we talk about counselling and 'talking to someone' as a viable option shows how far from an inter-cultural health system we really are. With few (sometimes no) black counsellors working in universities across the country, this provides another huge barrier to addressing the mental health problems of black women. I always took comfort when I didn't have to *explain* why I thought something was racist. My black friends just knew it, and most had experienced the exact same feelings. But your friends shouldn't have to be a last-resort option.

**You can't just give any counsellor to anyone. You will be telling your [white] counsellor things and she will be thinking, 'Why are you upset? This is not a big deal' . . . It puts you off wanting to even seek help in the first place,**

**which is a big step to take: to admit that you need help. – Mikai**

Micha, who was previously Cambridge Student Union's Welfare and Rights Officer, played a significant role in ensuring that for the first time, black and minority ethnic students could request to see BME counsellors. In pushing for the change, she found that words such as 'explaining', 'lecturing' and 'teaching' came up more than once in students' testimonials, demonstrating how therapy can quickly slip into providing emotional and educational labour just to get your therapist on the 'same page as you'. Students also found that they were 'routinely questioned about the validity and accuracy' of their experiences of racism.

**When I had CBT [Cognitive Behavioural Therapy] last year, a lot of the problems I had [were in] telling my CBT counsellor, who was a white man. I was like, a lot of the problems I have [are], you know, racism, sexism, that [affect] my mental health, so you know, it means I can't really make friends. And his answer was, 'Go to more society events, *make friends*.' – Fope**

A general approach to mental health is not the best way to tackle the growing crisis. Marginalised groups, such as black women, will continue to be misaddressed by health services that are racialised. It is virtually impossible to disentangle structures such as race, class, gender, disability and sexuality from mental health. Individuals such as Dr Isha McKenzie-Mavinga, an integrative transcultural psychotherapist, recognise this, and actively try to carve out safe places for black women to share their experiences and 'not feel mad and isolated'. Using the term 'black empathic approach', McKenzie-Mavinga has created a safe space in which black women's experiences are not denied but are validated. Similarly, the Black, African and Asian Therapy Network (BAATN) helps to connect BAME people with counsellors of the same or similar ethnic origin.

Alternatively, first points of call may become lecturers or personal and academic tutors, who are immediately more accessible to students. This pushes the point that understandings of mental health need to extend beyond the student in an academic sense. There is often a disconnect between what is happening on campuses and what is happening in classrooms. Those who work at universities – lecturers, professors, personal tutors and support staff – regularly encounter students in distress, yet this is largely removed from the conversation of mental health.

A study completed by Student Minds found that 'responding to student mental health problems now appears to be an inevitable part of the role of an academic' – academics being 'all staff employed to teach, supervise or tutor students in a university'. It revealed that when some academics encountered mental health problems in a student, they were able to notify the relevant student services team. However, responses to this were 'variable'. Crucially, 'there were differences of opinion around what constitutes a crisis and the urgency with which students should receive formal support'. The majority of staff are unsure about the fine line between moral and professional duties which bind staff to reporting or recommending formal support. All of this ties into a wider safeguarding question of whether academics should have a duty to report incidents, and whether current guidelines are adequate. Yet it is clear from the Student Minds report that students are becoming more reliant on academics, especially those with whom they come into contact every week. With the alleviation of immediate pressures, you can manage your workload, shift deadlines and plead mitigating circumstances if needed.

I found the idea of speaking to an academic hard. I didn't want them to pity me, or to give anyone any reason to suggest that I couldn't cope with university life. I didn't want my blackness to be misconstrued into a form of weakness, so in typical black-woman style, I coerced myself into silence. How could I possibly tell the very people who let me in that I was struggling to keep up? Or that I truly believed that they had made a mistake in accepting me into university?

**It would have been nice to have a black woman to speak to. This isn't to say that because she's a black woman we're going to have the same experiences because we're black, because I hate putting black people in boxes like that, but she might have been able to relate. – Adaobi**

It shouldn't be assumed that BME friends, counsellors, therapists or academics will automatically understand our personal traumas. A black male counsellor may be able to relate to the racial strife of black people, but not necessarily how ideas of patriarchy intersect with race. Nonetheless, where professional help is available, using it to the best of our ability is a sure advantage. As shown by Micha's efforts, the act of introducing BAME counsellors is a huge step towards addressing issues of the inclusivity of black students within universities.

### Self-Care 101

Besides counselling and university services, self-care includes taking productive steps to improving your lifestyle. The day after coffeegate, my neighbour Holly offered to walk forty-five minutes into town with me, as I was still too shaken to cycle to our American history lecture that morning, extreme sports helmet or no extreme sports helmet. We took the scenic route through the meadow, and tried to tactically dodge the cows in the middle of the path. Most importantly, she encouraged me to unpack my anxiety attack, and then was kind enough to share her own experiences with mental health. Don't get me wrong – the panic attacks didn't magically stop. But I learnt the best ways to manage them, and the positive steps I took after that day made my university experience a lot more pleasant.

Managing my anxiety at university was about pinpointing the main stressors and alleviating that stress as much as possible. If that meant unapologetically saying no, changing deadlines and putting myself first, then so be it. Mental health is important. Don't do what I did, and delay in addressing it.

**To survive every single day in that environment is always going to be a struggle. So, self-care is like having a plant and keeping it alive. – Arenike**

Your university room is likely to be pretty basic: desk, lamp, cupboard. It can feel impersonal and temporary at best, a little institutional at worst. At a time at which everything seemed to be strange and bewildering, bringing items from home helped me create my home away from home. By items, I mean *anything*. Before we left home, I would scavenge bits of wrapping paper, raid old family photo albums, and pile up my favourite throws and blankets. I forced my dad and my older brother to find space in the car for my fluffy red carpet, fairy lights and giant vanity mirror. It was quite a sight watching them lug everything in to my room. I would dedicate the first day of term to organising the furniture and furnishings, before venturing out in search of Blu-tac and a cute house plant or two. I stuck up photographs of my family and friends from home, especially all the important black women in my life, like my mum and my sister, and surrounded their faces with quotes and Ankara fabric. Whenever I felt low or down, going to my room always picked me up. I felt I wasn't alone.

**I never had pictures up, not even a plant, not even a candle. Like, my friends used to come over all the time and be like, *not even a cheeky fairy light?* What's a fairy light? No, I want to lay my head, get up and go. Like it did not feel like home. I loved having my own space, but it wasn't home. I didn't feel settled in. – Courtney**

Taking time to settle in to your new space can make a real difference in adjusting to university life – but even when your room is perfectly decorated, it can still feel as if something is missing. There was a general consensus among everyone we interviewed that surrounding yourself with not only familiar items, but also with people who are like you, online and offline, was crucial to maintaining good mental health.

**This is what we say in every BAME network at the beginning of each session: 'Find your tribe.' – Fope**

Sometimes, self-care just means protecting yourself from environments and people who you might find harmful. The moments you feel energised and alive will be with people who you can relate to the most. This doesn't have to be only one group; different groups or 'tribes' can serve different purposes in your life. In particular, online spaces have become invaluable for black women. In real life, there are not many safe spaces for us to meet, socialise, vent or simply have candid conversations. Black women around the world are waiting and eager to be connected, and to learn about each other's experiences. Finding your tribe is also about listening to the experiences of older black women, who are accessible thanks to the internet. Through common struggles, jokes and trends, there's something reassuring about knowing there's someone out there who looks like you *and* feels the same as you do. When asked where she found refuge at university, this is what Mikai had to say:

> **On YouTube! With my subscribers. On Instagram when I be writing those long [posts], when my head is going to fall off and my dissertation is coming to kill me everyone will be commenting, 'Same, sis!'**

Listening to podcasts was revolutionary for me when it came to discovering other online spaces. Schedule at least one hour a day when you can be still, listen and take on helpful tips. You can skip around and find topics that are most relevant to you. The 'Therapy for Black Girls' podcast is a weekly conversation with psychologist Dr Joy Harden Bradford. Also, Oprah's 'SuperSoul' podcast is designed to 'guide you through life's big questions and help bring you one step closer to your best self'. For around an hour, just listening to someone else talk, laugh and debate was enough to temporarily stop my thoughts. I didn't need to be stressed or feel particularly down to listen to podcasts, but found it a useful way to wind down and disconnect for a bit. By the end of term, I didn't care if the whole corridor could hear me screaming or laughing at Tolly T, Audrey, formally known as Ghana's Finest, and Mamacita Milena

Sanchez on the podcast 'The Receipts'. The girls have carved out their own online haven for women of colour, who have the opportunity to listen to conversations that are unapologetic and open. From 'The struggle is real but not necessary' to 'Role models and the price of virginity', it's like being in a WhatsApp group chat with people who feel like your older sisters.

Another outlet, you might be surprised to learn, is self-care apps. We're regularly told that the key to mental wellbeing and vitality is staying away from our phones and limiting our screen time. I agree that mindless scrolling and scrutinising the lifestyles of others can be really unhelpful when you're trying to focus on what is best for yourself. But downloading an app meant that self-care didn't have to be expensive or complicated; it also made information accessible, anywhere and anytime.

The Student Health App is free, and was founded by experienced doctors who want to support the self-care of students, 'which is about avoiding disease, maintaining health, handling illness and disability'. Bristol, UCL, Lady Margaret Hall at Oxford and St Andrews have partnered with the app. It provides a personalised service for students; with a click of a button, you're directed to your university's helplines and services. It's just one way of addressing the need for mental health services, at least preventative measures, to be more accessible. Apps like Headspace, the @tinycarebot on Twitter and Daylio are some other personal favourites that act as light reminders to address your mental health every day – not just when you're feeling low.

\*

But sometimes decorating your room or finding a suitable app isn't enough. One of the questions I asked our interviewees was whether they ever felt like dropping out. Here's what some of them said.

**Oh, only every day. Every single day. – Mikai**

**No, I'll be honest and say no. I'm really grateful for that. – Eireann**

**I felt like I wanted to drop out, but I knew I never would. I was going to change universities, but I was never going to drop out of university completely. – Kenya**

Personally, I really didn't think it was an option to take time out. Practically speaking, I didn't know anything about how I would even go about doing it. I was only familiar with taking a year out before university (gap yah) to have a short break before going back into education. It was only once I got to university that I heard of intermitting. The process of intermitting (sometimes referred to as intercalating) is designed to allow students to have a temporary break from studies for medical or non-medical reasons. It serves to reinforce the idea that university isn't going anywhere, despite being under the constant impression that we have to do things to a strict timeline.

Students have worked hard to make this process more transparent and ensure that support systems, such as providing a smooth transition back into university life, are in place for those who do decide to take a break from their studies. It offers a compromise, in that you don't have to completely drop out, but you can accept that your mental state or current situation is not conducive to you doing your best.

University self-care is fundamentally about striking a work-life balance. Learn to relax over any weekends, breaks, holidays or vacations you have away from the university environment. Time away is crucial to recouping your energy. Whether that means sleeping for a week straight, or taking part in hobbies or sports, it's a chance for you to do something that makes *you* feel good – because no one else will do it for you. Self-care doesn't have to be a sudden action that dramatically changes your life. Instead, slowly building on something you achieved yesterday and the days before can offer a big win.

Try and have a good time. Even if that does mean sacking off your work sometimes and taking a decent long nap. 'Cos that is fun, believe me. – Nathania

No one's going to kill you for going for a cheeky cider. – Barbara

## Thinking Out Loud

University is a trying time, and the transition may or may not drain you. Especially when you're a black girl in a predominately white institution, your resilience will be slowly chipped away. Self-care will be a somewhat radical attempt to put yourself first. Not everyone will understand – and that doesn't matter. Most of the time, if you have mental health issues you don't want to have to constantly drag up deep and personal anecdotes all the time. Similarly, the onus shouldn't *always* be on you to 'speak up'. Instead, there needs to be a wider conversation about how and why the wider university system fails to incorporate student wellbeing into its fundamental structure.

You may be in a position where you don't have any existing issues with your mental health, or won't experience any at university. Where possible, ask how to help, and offer to be available for support to those around you who are experiencing issues. But never lose sight of the fact that prioritising your own mental health is more important. It may seem like a basic thing to say, but just as you have to pay attention to your physical health, you should do the same for your mental health. If you're in bed with the flu, you wouldn't go for a ten-mile run, you'd go to the doctor. If you're feeling particularly stressed or anxious, don't push yourself to work even harder – seek out someone to speak to about it, and give yourself a break. Never feel that you're alone. Everyone has to maintain their mental health to some degree. For me, this has meant that charting the good days is equally as important as charting the bad ones.

It may well be, though, that 'self-care' tips are hard to implement – especially if you're at crisis point. Little is said about mental health disorders such as bipolar disorder, psychosis and mania, and borderline personality disorders. We need to ask whether mental health conversations are truly becoming more open – or whether it's only those around anxiety and depression that are becoming more open. For most, mental health problems do not come in smooth, pre-packaged, manageable bouts. It's often irregular feelings of intense highs and extreme lows. Nothing in this chapter should be a substitute for seeking professional or medical advice and help.

Universities should not be seen as places only of education and academic excellence. They should utilise their positions to promote resources that help develop healthy students, staff and the wider community. Students across all universities have worked incredibly hard to address gaping holes in mental health provision. There really is no excuse. Students create the fabric of university life and therefore should be valued in a holistic sense.

## 4

## *Finding Spaces*

Ọrẹ

Before I came to university, I had heard plenty about the infamous 'Freshers' Week'. Freshers' week refers to the first week (or few days) of university, during which a series of social events are planned by student groups to help first years, or freshers, mingle.

I had seen all my brother's pictures from his freshers' week at Newcastle, and heard about the foam parties, bar crawls and random fancy dress events. Freshers' week was sold to me as 'organised fun' that would be an interesting yet essential part of my university experience. I expected it to be where I would make my first and best friends, bond with everyone that I lived with, and consume copious amounts of alcohol that I knew I would later regret. Although I was nervous, the prospect of complete independence, with what seemed like no rules, excited me.

Luckily, I had made a few friends before I started university. At my college interview, I had met and befriended Alex, who had also got a place; he became my first friend – and eventually one of my best friends in those three years. We relied on each other for sanity in exam season and lifted each other up when the work got relentless. But Alex wasn't the only friend I had been lucky enough to meet before university. Chelsea and I have a cute love story too. At a careers event for 'high-achieving' black students in the weeks before we started university, I got busy networking with black students headed to universities across the country. On the way home, a group of us girls walked to the tube station together. Chelsea was one of them, and we began to talk about how scared we were to start Cambridge. We swapped numbers, as she was getting on the tube in the other direction, and for the next few days, we made plans ahead of freshers' week. We planned outfits, discussed where we were going to find plantain and looked for Cambridge hairstylists that could help us touch up our braids during term time.

But five days before I was due to start university, disaster struck. I was home alone in the kitchen. I had made a pot of jollof rice and another pot of chicken stew. After seeing a good deal on plantain outside West Croydon station, I said to myself, why not fry some plantain on the side? I got a bit excited in the kitchen, and whacked the whole pan of blazing hot oil and plantain onto both of my thighs. After waiting two hours for an ambulance, my neighbour put me in a cab to A&E with bad subdermal burns. The doctors ordered that I was to be in and out of hospital for two weeks. I managed to hobble up to Cambridge and into university for my college matriculation photo and a sexual consent workshop. But for the most part, my highly anticipated freshers' week was cancelled. I was distraught.

As it turned out, apparently I didn't miss much.

**[Freshers' week was] everything that I could imagine but ten times worse. – Kenya**

**I remember I cried. Loads. I was super, super worried about friends. I really didn't meet many people that I thought I got on really well with. – Micha**

**Oh my gosh, the memory of freshers' week makes me feel sick. It was objectively one of the worst things I've ever gone through in my entire life. – Renée**

**I went out once, came back really early and have never been to a party again. – Adaobi**

During freshers' week, some people have fun. Everyone else puts on a brave face and *acts* like they're having fun. Most people are terribly homesick, struggling to deal with their newfound independence, missing their old friends who are now spread to all four corners of the country, and surrendering themselves to an experience that for the most part is terribly awkward. In student forums online, many students will tell you that freshers' week is filled with 'lots of booze and sex' – and just as many will tell you that this is an overplayed stereotype and really isn't the case. Either way, most students agree that they only made their real friends in the weeks that followed.

However, even in those weeks afterwards, I personally still found it quite hard to settle into university. To try and fit in, and to catch up on missing freshers' week, I found myself engaging in habits that were very unlike me, simply because it felt as if that was what everyone else at university was doing. I would go to clubs with music that I hated and hang around the smoking areas (though I don't even smoke), having really long conversations with strangers in the freezing cold. Then I would head back to college, stinking of smoke and battling a cough. Nothing about it was enjoyable for me, but I would do it again and again, because I was led to believe that was the only way people were making friends. After weeks of this uncomfortable ritual, I still felt really lonely. It wasn't that the people I met weren't *nice* – but I just didn't think that they were my kind of people. I was looking for all the other black girls that I could stick to, who would stick up for me, and who would tell me that they could relate to what I was feeling. I remember telling my friends from home that I could die in my room and no one would know for days. I didn't feel that I had met anyone who genuinely cared about me.

Imposter syndrome, and the broader feeling that you are inadequate, is something that most students will experience in the early days. Pauline Clance and Suzanne Imes, the psychologists who coined the term, describe it as the 'internal experience of intellectual phoniness in people who believe that they are not intelligent, capable or creative despite evidence of high achievement'. While imposter syndrome is something that most students feel to some degree, you suffer from it uniquely when you are also made to stand out by your status as a racial minority. Your feeling like an 'imposter' is made visible, reinforced by the relative absence of people who look like you. A 2013 study by a group of American psychologists revealed that feelings of stress and minority-related depression in education were highest in black students. It's only in hindsight that I can understand that I was dealing with something similar. I was constantly censoring myself, having to be someone else in order to have a chance of being accepted. I felt that in order to thrive in this new university space, I would have to leave my full self – my *black* self – at the door. Only later would I realise how much of an emotional toll this had taken on me.

While it's common for those dealing with imposterism to struggle alone and in silence, I would learn from the friends I later made that I was not the only one feeling this, and that many had it worse than I did. These feelings of imposterism and minority-related depression manifest even more for black working-class students, who are marginalised by both their racial and class identities.

**When I got to university, it was the task of juggling a sense of belonging in a very middle-to-upper-class higher education system and still existing in a working-class home that completely threw me. – Chelsea.**

While Chelsea was struggling on a student loan that almost always fell short every term, she would overhear other students talking about how they had spent over £600 in a month on brunch. For her, class was as significant an obstacle as race when it came to settling in. It exacerbated her experience of imposter syndrome, and she found herself retreating from university and college life.

If you've never really left a big city before, you may be surprised to discover that very few places in the UK have the same level of diversity as London, Manchester or Birmingham. Moving far away may mean that you're separated from those aspects of your culture that were so central to your life before university. To make up for the friends I had not made at Cambridge, I found myself going back to London (I will personally fight anyone who tells me Croydon is not in London) every week or two to see my old friends. I constantly felt the need to escape, to be in spaces where I could be my full self, not whatever weird version of myself I was trying to be in those early days at university.

At last, one evening in my second term, I had a long conversation with three people who would go on to become some of my best friends at university. After that conversation, I cried – and then called my mum, telling her that I had found my people, that for the first time I felt that if I died in my room, these were people who would care enough to check up on me. It was at this point that I felt I had finally settled in.

### Fitting In

There is a lot of drinking at university. A *lot*. A whopping 79 per cent of respondents to a 2018 survey by the National Union of Students (NUS) said that drinking is a part of university culture. When you arrive at university, it may feel that everyone's idea of fun is to get really drunk, go clubbing, rinse and repeat. 'Pre-drinks', house parties and student nights at clubs are the main form of socialising, especially in the early days. And by drinking I don't just mean the odd glass of wine – it was more commonly situations like drinking beer out of a pipe attached to a keg and then spinning around several times until you vomited. And then going again. Arriving at lectures with hangovers is normalised, if not glamorised.

Young adults are the most likely age group to binge on alcohol (according to the Office for National Statistics), and this is partly due to drinking cultures at universities. We used the 'work hard, play hard' mantra to justify our alcohol intake in the new high-pressure environment of university, but for many, alcohol becomes not only a way to relax but an increasingly-turned-to means of coping with the challenges.

Drinking is so central to life at some universities that there are societies that revolve around it. I was in an all-girls drinking society at my college, the Black Widows. Historically, 'exclusive' drinking societies at Oxford and Cambridge such as the Bullingdon Club and the Pitt Club have been reserved for the wealthiest white, male students (David Cameron and Boris Johnson were both members of Oxford's Bullingdon Club). Most drinking societies are known for being very exclusionary, and allowing only people who went to private schools to be members. They are institutions that represent a marker of social privileges across identity groups and another context in which male privilege at university is perpetuated. I accepted an invitation to join the Black Widows at the end of my first year because it seemed like yet another opportunity to socialise and actually make some friends in my college and across the university. In events called 'swaps', female drinking societies and male drinking societies would go out to dinner together, and would aim to get as drunk as possible through drinking games and challenges. Although I never encountered such vile situations myself, the stories of sexual harassment, bullying, classism and racism in many other drinking societies make it clear that they are problematic. In the spring of 2018, a Cambridge-based Facebook page, known for anonymous submissions, became dedicated to exposing drinking societies, publishing the accounts of victims of bullying and sexual misconduct within them. People shared their horror stories, with some saying their drinks had been spiked, and others complaining about incidents in which male societies sang chants about rape.

While I soon realised that drinking societies weren't exactly my idea of fun, I still loved going clubbing, and I found out that there was more than one way to go about enjoying nightlife (and drinking) at university. I found a night called 'Fleek Fridays' that played all the Afrobeats and RnB that I wanted to hear. The friends who would turn up with me on most Fridays soon followed. It effectively became the 'black music' night and I loved it. I needed it.

We cannot ignore, though, that clubs are yet another place in which everyday racism manifests. It's not uncommon to hear stories of black students not being allowed into certain clubs, being randomly selected for bag searches, or even being followed by security. In 2017, a group of black students were refused entry to a nightclub in Cardiff because the club management didn't want an 'urban feel' to their club.

It doesn't always get much better when you are inside. Some nights are fun, and I have an incredible archive of Snapchat memories from my university years to testify to that. You're getting lit with your friends, catching all your whines, gassing your girls up when they're killing it on the dancefloor, and so on. But on other nights, the racist realities of the world permeate the club scene and turn a good night sour.

> **Clubbing was a massive source of upset and [discomfort] and something that made me feel really alienated in Cambridge. I remember going out with blonde friends who would get hit on by guys, and just feeling both undesirable and invisible, like you didn't even exist in this space. – Micha**

The constant reminders that no one was interested in you became draining. I can count on one hand the number of times I went out clubbing and a guy approached me. In a social context in which it seems as if lots of relationships are being forged, especially in the early days, this can be disheartening. It will be a frequent reminder of what it means as a black girl to not fall into society's standards of desirable.

Often, when you *are* approached, it's by people so in awe of your blackness that they fetishise you. Renee spoke to me about how 'creative' guys can get with their pickup lines:

> **There's 'brown sugar', all sorts of nonsense . . . I think the funniest one was 'chocolate mocha princess' . . . Like, sir, I just came to enjoy my martini in peace.**

*Chocolate mocha princess*?! While Renée laughs about it in hindsight, constantly being compared to food by drunk boys in the club can be exhausting. The ones who may not compare you to something edible may opt instead for the 'you're fit for a black girl' line or even, 'I've never been with a black girl before.' You are not some kind of experience or adventurous option to be tried. While I advise you to ignore these comments as best you can, rest assured I know how easily they can ruin your night.

*

The ubiquity of alcohol in university social spaces can be particularly isolating for people who don't drink. The NUS in 2018 asked universities to introduce more 'inclusive spaces' for teetotal students on campus because the centrality of drinking can be difficult to escape. Most student events, especially things like bar crawls in freshers' week, fall short when it comes to fully accommodating teetotal students. In addition to being excluded from certain events, these students often find themselves being quizzed by their peers on the reasons behind their sobriety.

**I don't drink because I think alcohol tastes dis-gusting. But it was weird because people just don't get why you don't drink. I didn't ever feel**

**pressure to drink but I had friends who did feel like they had to drink to belong. – Ayomide**

It is very possible to survive university without drinking. There will be hundreds of societies and other spaces that have a range of ways to keep you busy; I'll explore some of these spaces in the rest of this chapter. And if you do choose to go clubbing, find the nights you like. Don't end up like me, who spent a whole year dancing to dead Disney tunes two nights a week before I realised there were clubs that I liked and DJs that played all the Wizkid I needed to hear.

Unless you've been to boarding school, university is probably the first time you'll be living with a whole bunch of people your own age – and it will get messy. Most universities will offer you accommodation (in your first year, at least). On the one hand, this could be convenient – on the other, you will probably have little choice as to who you get to live with. If you're lucky, you'll get on with everyone in your halls of residence, but chances are, it won't always be bliss. For starters, I advise that you don't keep your plantain in the communal fridge just in case an unaware housemate mistakes it for a mouldy banana and throws it in the bin. True story, guys, I kid you not. You may also have to share bathrooms with people who don't know how to make good use of a toilet brush.

You will probably bump into your housemates on a daily basis (maybe weekly basis if you're particularly good at staying away from communal areas), and the proximity may make them convenient friends to have. However, living situations can also be a massive source of upset, socially speaking – and so if you find yourself feeling a bit left out, you're not alone, because I did too.

If you go to a university with a collegiate system, like Cambridge, Oxford, Durham and York, you'll find that roughly speaking, your academic life is controlled by your university departments or faculties, while everything social and residential is run by your college. We were told by other students that most of our friends would come from our college. It seemed to be true, for the most part. Everyone I lived with was buddying up. I couldn't understand why I was struggling to integrate. I just found college more isolating as time went on.

**Cambridge really sells this idea of, you socialise in your college, or college is like your family. But I was the only black girl in my college for like three years. It's really, really hard, and it doesn't feel like a family. Towards the end of second year, I realised I didn't have to subscribe to the whole college lifestyle . . . I didn't have to keep being reminded that I was a minority. – Arenike**

There's nothing wrong with seeking out other options if life in college, or with people in your halls, isn't for you. In fact, I found that some of the most comfortable places for me were outside my college, in societies that I sought out on my own, where I found people who shared my feelings of isolation and minority representation.

## Making Space

Some people have taken it upon themselves to respond to these feelings of isolation by making spaces of their own. For Saskia, this began in Cambridge's theatre world, which for a long time had been **'really white and inaccessible'** and **'a boys' club of nepotism'**, they told me. Despite having done no acting before university, the lack of accessibility for people of colour and non-private school students inspired them to start a Cambridge BME Theatre group on Facebook. Saskia eventually went on to direct many BME-only cast plays in Cambridge. Their first BME-only cast production, *Macbeth*, sold out every performance except the matinee.

> **Almost every show I've ever done is a refuge. I did Fences in my final year, and I've never seen so many black people in the audience for something before. It makes a massive difference to the atmosphere. It's so special. – Saskia**

Another example is Warwick's FlowSoc, created by Jeremiah Amoako-Gyapong:

> **'FlowSoc' was basically about music performance, poetry and spoken word. It was a lot of expressing yourself through creativity, and I**

**thought it was very useful in terms of finding people to connect with and people that could support you, through poetry or through singing or whatever. – Mikai**

For me, my refuge was my house. I would cook jollof rice or corned beef stew and invite all my favourite people round. Bonding over food that we loved and missed, food that played so much of a role in making up our cultural identities, was important. At home, we eat jollof at parties, with family and with friends. I would spend hours in the kitchen perfecting the dish, and I loved that I could recreate such an important space for people at university. We would laugh and cry about everything from relationships to school work until the early hours of the morning, before the reality of the next day's lectures reared its head. Being surrounded by people I loved, and people whom I felt truly loved me, gave me all the fire that I needed to get by. The solidarity that I found in such relationships was essential, the conversations we had unforgettable, and it's one of the things I miss the most about Cambridge.

Some people find that solidarity in online spaces too. Fope gave me some insight into how powerful online spaces can be:

**I used to moderate a group called Radical Black and Brown Hotties [RBBH], which had over 2,000 members at its peak. There's RBBH Brighton, Berlin, London and France. I know people who have started dating from the group and people who have definitely made friends from the group. They've even helped me write essays.**

Online spaces are crucial, especially for marginalised communities. Facebook groups and black Twitter networks have been a central hub for both socialising *and* organising. They have been important sites for education and progressive conversations, away from those complicit in oppression. At Cambridge, we had a network called 'FLY', which was created to encourage this kind of solidarity. FLY, which I learned stands for 'Freedom. Love. You.', is a forum for women and non-binary people of colour (WNBPOC) to advise, support, or just listen, through an online Facebook group. It was created by BME women before us and has continued to be an important space for women and non-binary people of colour at Cambridge. FLY held weekly meetings in which WNBPOC from across the university could get together and be reminded that our experiences are valid.

**I went to FLY a lot, which was revolutionary for me. It kind of weirdly reminds me of having therapy at uni. – Micha**

**It was an incredible opportunity to talk to people who have been in your exact position, about this essay that you can't do, and which clubs to go to, and how to navigate Cambridge as a person of colour. – Saskia**

Warwick's Anti-Racism Society, or WARSoc, is another example of a society that aims to provide a safe space for its members. Other such spaces include sexual assault survivor groups, disability groups and mental health groups. Safe spaces like these are heavily criticised for 'undermining free speech', but that's far from the point. They are a sanctuary in which minorities can engage in discourse without being silenced, places in which we are allowed to prioritise our own life experiences and histories of oppression, amid a society that often glosses over them. We can exhale, and find comfort in the knowledge that other people share these experiences; we are not alone.

However, it is important to bear in mind that not everyone has similar ideas of what safety looks or feels like. While for many, safe spaces allow us to be protected from the damaging opinions of communities that oppress us, they can also make it harder to disagree with those you share the space with.

**I didn't like the hypocrisy. A lot of the time it was, 'You agree with our opinion or you're wrong' – and that to me is such a dangerous thing to do in a safe space. – Courtney**

Safe spaces are useful and necessary, and this criticism should not undermine their importance. But for me, it was the first time that I realised that woman-of-colour solidarity is not a given, and that I could forgive myself for not feeling safe in a space where it seemed other black girls did. I say this for the other black women who have felt similarly isolated. A room full of other women sharing their experiences of racism may not be your idea of safety and solidarity, and you are allowed to feel that. FLY, like many other safe spaces, was an important source of education, therapy and refuge, and although it didn't quite work for me, there were other spaces that did. I came to realise that different societies served different purposes for me.

*

**Without ACS, I don't know how I would have survived. – Courtney**

Whatever university you go to, you will find a society for almost every activity under the sun (we even had a

Quidditch Society* at Cambridge). Societies are helpful for fostering a smaller sense of community with people who share your interests. However, a special mention goes out to the cultural societies that offer BME students a second home at university through events dedicated to sharing and celebrating their cultural communities. I found the ACS at Cambridge to be this and more.

I first encountered my university's ACS in November of my first year when I went to an event called 'Culture Fest'. There was jollof rice, music and spoken word performances, and lots of people were in traditional dress. Suddenly, I didn't feel I was in Cambridge any more. In fact, everything that seemed to make me stick out in the rest of Cambridge helped me fit right in. My first reaction was, 'Where have all these black people been hiding?' I was in a place where people understood all my cultural references, and shared my histories and, very importantly, my taste in music! I had found a society in Cambridge that felt like home. I went to almost every weekly ACS event that followed, from the parties to the talks – even the Valentine's Day 'Take Me Out'.

---

* It's that game they played in Harry Potter on the flying broomsticks. I cannot confirm that flying brooms are included in the society's membership.

The ACS is run by a small committee of elected students. I admired the group that had had such an impact on me and given me hope that I could truly enjoy Cambridge. In my second year, I decided to run for Events Officer, because I wanted to contribute to someone else's ACS experience and be more involved in what seemed to be a meaningful family.

**I saw people who looked like me, and we could dance to Vybz Kartel and then talk about feminism. – Nathania**

Being on the ACS Committee was . . . interesting. ACS committee drama seemed to be a thing everywhere, but we had it quite bad. We inherited a huge debt from our predecessors, and within three months, our president kicked someone off the committee. Halfway through the year, the president then resigned, for reasons that were not revealed to the rest of us. In spite of the pretty tempestuous start, under new leadership we managed to raise lots of sponsorship money, and even hold our first-ever ACS ball.

Most British universities have an ACS in some capacity. They're a particularly significant means for black students to engage with their own institutions and other universities. You may encounter events such as the 'Great Debate Tour' or the dance competition 'Big Clash', which involve many university ACSs. ACSs also have the potential to be an important political force, since they are the closest that we have to a country-wide black students union (especially since the NUS's 'Black Students Campaign' represents everyone who is 'politically black', or non-white). ACSs are generally known for having great parties and food, and embodying black British culture and diasporic identity within university life. Many corporate firms have noticed the value of these societies, and provide sponsorship to ACSs in the hope that black graduates will be attracted to their firms in the future. We would work for weeks perfecting shiny sponsorship proposals, detailing how many members we had, how much we had grown and how much we needed these corporations' help to keep that growth going.

Cambridge ACS is a bit different from other ACSs across the country in some respects. Having a very small black community meant that we often couldn't match what other ACSs were doing because we didn't have the manpower. We would look enviously at places like Warwick, which had a black community so large that both their ACS and their Nigerian Society could afford to throw huge balls every year. The more I met with black people from other universities, though, the more it became clear that this lack of black students wasn't only a Cambridge problem. Some universities don't even have enough black people willing to form an ACS committee. It was upsetting to learn that even though ACS had become so important to me, some people at other universities would never know what that felt like.

At the end of my second year, I ran for ACS president. I knew that there was nothing else that I would rather give my energy to for a whole year. I had become so invested in seeing this society grow because I saw how important it was for so many black people.

> **I think ACS will always come first. If I had to drop anything else for it, I would. I really give a shit about our community. – Nathania**

I had come to learn that although many ACSs in the UK are broadly about socialising, networking and getting black people into corporate jobs, Cambridge ACS *had* to be political in its aims.

> **Our ACS is inherently quite political because being black at Cambridge is political. – Chelsea**

For example, we had to address the fact Cambridge had an access problem and that black students were under-represented. The university's most recent admissions statistics revealed that twenty-seven black men and thirty-three black women were accepted in 2017. While this is an improvement on the year of my intake, black applicants still have a lower *success* rate than white applicants. Essentially this means that even though more black people are applying, they are still less likely to receive an offer and then meet its terms. To counter this very specific problem, we introduced mentoring schemes and access conferences for black secondary school students. The goal was to pour all the knowledge we had about the process into potential black candidates so that they were better prepared and well-equipped not only to apply to Cambridge, but also to get in.

The increasing politicisation of ACSs seems to be a wider phenomenon. In my time at university, we were beginning to see many more ACSs hosting important discussions about black mental health and misogynoir; some were introducing LGBTQ+ officers to assist in the fight against homophobia and transphobia that often plague black communities. The ACS was *my* sanctuary, and I strongly recommend that black students at least give it a go while at university. You may have to pay a small membership fee to join – between £10 and £30 at most universities - but the memories I made were worth way more than the money.

Some people still felt isolated within this society, though. The focus on partying can exclude people who don't enjoy that kind of nightlife, or those who are more introverted. As is the case with many black spaces in the diaspora, ACSs tend to be dominated by West Africans, and particularly Nigerians, and many non-Nigerian black people often had a harder time identifying with that reality. ACSs need to make a more conscious effort to counter the overrepresentation of Nigerians in their societies – and I say that as a Nigerian who has been complicit in, and profited from, this overrepresentation! As an African-*Caribbean* Society, we have a duty to make sure that Caribbeans are also fairly represented.

The obsession with getting black students into corporate jobs in the city is one that is bigger than a student society. Yet we still have a responsibility to make sure that black students who want to pursue alternative career paths are equally supported. While it is the price that we pay for the corporate sponsorships that we receive, it reinforces the notion that there is only one path to success as a black graduate.

So yes, there's work to be done. But I know that the joy that I felt in this society was like nothing that I found anywhere else at university.

*

While I made myself at home socially in the ACS, I found a spiritual home in my Cambridge church. As a Christian, I hopped from church to church in my first year, trying to find what worked for me. Although I was born in a Christian household and have gone to church since I was a child, I made the personal decision to give my life to Christ early on in university. I was looking for somewhere where I would feel moved by the spirit, somewhere that reminded me of the churches that I was used to, but also somewhere that would support me in my baby Christian journey. I found it quite difficult to stay on my Christian path, especially in my first year, because I was in an academic environment that relied so much on proving everything, explaining everything and justifying everything. It seemed at odds with being Christian, which relies on faith that you can't really explain.

**When you're in academic spaces, there's always an excuse of why God doesn't exist or why it's irrational to believe in God . . . but then I felt very lonely at university. – Courtney**

By my second year, I had finally settled into a church which I loved. It was, I came to find, yet another community that reminded me of home. We would sing songs of praise that I had been singing since I was a child, the pastor was Nigerian and a lot of the congregation shared my background. It was a community that welcomed me with open arms, and it became a great comfort when university work really began to take its toll. Sometimes I would go to church and cry a little bit, and then I was good. It was a different kind of escape, a very personal one for me, and I don't think my friends really knew or understood why I needed it so much.

> **When I've not read my Bible in a long time, which happens a lot, it's just nice to always know that you can pray it will be fine. – Ayomide**

Saredo is a Muslim, and found similar solace in religion while at university:

> **I always found religion was just a very personal thing. When it comes to faith, it's kind of letting you know that there is a path, whether or not I felt like I was on that path: in times of struggle and times of uncertainty, instead of seeing or viewing it as everything falling apart, just seeing it as everything coming together.**

When you're homesick, or thinking about dropping out, or feeling like you have no one, a call from someone that they're praying for you might help. It was yet another support system that I didn't know I needed. I met people who would send me messages to check on me when I had exams coming up, or who would make sure I was okay if I had missed church for a few weeks.

**I found a church and I met a lady, Aunty Sunk-anmi. She took my number and she took me under her wing and it was like having a mother figure at university . . . She was constantly check-ing up on me and making me food. – Courtney**

If you're a person of faith, find ways to keep that faith at university despite the pressure to explain why you believe what you believe. Church helped me stay grounded and was yet another comfort for me.

## The Idea of a Black Sisterhood

I am grateful that I found spaces in university that I could thrive in. It may have taken me a while to settle in and to find my groove, but once I did, places like the ones I have discussed here kept me going. The support and solidarity that I found fuelled my fire.

There appears to be a running narrative in the circles I move in that black girls don't do enough to support each other. I'm not convinced that is true.

**I always saw black girls really supporting each other in a way that was very unconditional. – Micha**

I am thankful for the black girls I found who just got it. They understood what I was going through without me having to explain. They would allow me to grow dependent on them, and they in turn on me, because we knew we needed each other. We would catch each other's eyes when we were the only black girls in the room, and feel the silent solidarity. They would understand exactly what about university was so difficult, and yet would also be the ones to try and make it a bit more bearable for you.

This whole book is written on exactly that premise: an inherent inclination to root for everyone black. It's a remarkable sisterhood that we're able to share in and that we should take pride in. So let's end that story here. Black girls do support each other, unapologetically so, and some of the greatest, most durable black sisterhoods will be formed in the trying times of university.

However, I question whether the idea that we *should* support and befriend every black girl ever is a fair expectation. One thing I wish I had learnt before I started university was that I could be both passionate about the importance of black spaces and the need for black girl solidarity, without feeling an obligation to be best friends with every black girl I encountered. In the first term, one black girl made a WhatsApp group for every black girl in our year which, I thought, was a clever idea. However, with time, it became clear that some of us didn't get along. The group offered a false sense of unity that masked deeper issues. I think I was mistaken, as were many others in the group, into thinking that we would all be friends by default.

**It's interesting how we live in a climate [where] black women feel the need to always support each other, and I say this because when we got to Cambridge, there were a lot of black girls I just**

**simply didn't like. You're now stuck in this middle ground where, *I really don't like you, but I have to support you for the bigger cause* – which is a shame because you're not being genuine. – Chelsea**

While it is important to find spaces in which you can escape and exhale, don't force it. You have no obligation to befriend and support every individual just because they're black. I tolerated a lot more than I should have from black girls in leadership positions because I felt I had to. I didn't want to allow others to use our own conflict against us. I yearned for a united front that didn't always exist, because I knew that we had bigger fights to fight together. But what use is false solidarity? I learned that it's possible to both believe in the necessity of a broad solidarity among black girls without feeling forced to like each and every single one as an individual.

Even if you magically do get along with every other black girl you find at university, what's to say that you will have the extra energy and time to consistently support them?

**Black women have so much shit to deal with anyway. It's hard enough to just stay existing and surviving in a space like Cambridge. If you**

**don't have the extra energy to endlessly offer up labour to support other people, I think it's fair enough. – Micha**

**The Oxbridge context is tough because you're dealing with so much that it's hard to even check up on someone else. – Renée**

Lastly, don't let the fantasy of the black sisterhood fool you into thinking that the only people who will be there to support you will be black and female. For the sake of time and space, I have made gross generalisations about men and non-black people; there were certainly people looking out for me who were neither black nor female, but offered up relentless support.

I understand that supporting other black girls isn't always easy or possible. I understand that the obligation isn't completely fair. But I also understand how fulfilling it is to know that there are black girls out there rooting for you. I felt that way in these spaces, with many of my university friends-turned-family who still stand by me today. So, black girls: when you get to university, I hope you find spaces you feel comfortable in, help make them if they don't exist, and forge sisterhoods that will root for you.

5

## Desirability and Relationships

Chelsea

As daunting a prospect as university is, it is also a moment of exhilaration and liberation. We run away from the watchful eyes of our parents and family straight into an idealised playground of sweet *freedom*. You are granted your own space and your own schedule. You are surrounded by thousands of people your age and presented with the opportunity to meet and make friends with whoever you like. All of a sudden, you are master of your love life: free to test out romantic relationships without awkwardly having to sneak anyone into and out of your parents' house.

Dating at university can be life-changing for many students. Around 20 per cent of men and 18 per cent of women apparently find true love at university. The One Day University Love Survey stated that the top five universities in which to find that potential life-long partner are:

- Oxford (35 per cent of students)
- York (29 per cent)
- Durham (25 per cent)
- Liverpool (23 per cent)
- Manchester (21 per cent)

Now you all know where to apply if you want the best chance at finding long-term love. Call me Cupid Chelsea!

That's not to say that some people don't arrive at university already in relationships. I won't disguise the fact that maintaining existing relationships at university is hard and tiring, and requires a level of sacrifice few first-year students are able to commit to. I remember seeing a host of buzzing girlfriends helping settle their boyfriends in on the first day. Apart from a few heated arguments about missed twenty-minute FaceTime slots, I don't think I heard or saw any of them again.

Previous relationships withered away as people found that they couldn't maintain a degree *and* a relationship at the same time.

However, the dating scene for the majority of black girls at university is a minefield. To be honest, there isn't really much of a 'dating scene'; more, as Jasmine Lee-Zogbessou puts it, a 'dating puddle'. Despite carefully skirting around the people you definitely want to avoid, it's not long before you're hit with the reminder that ideas of desirability underline our very existence. Once you recognise this, it's hard to ignore the racism, misogynoir and prejudice that come with being black and seeking out relationships within university spaces.

The black female body has historically functioned as a scene of the doing and undoing of racial and gender-based structures of power. Representations and stereotypes of black women have been controlled by the media and society, who have served to reinforce a one-dimensional caricature. When we're not 'intimidating' and 'aggressive', we're 'hypersexual' and 'sassy'. We snap our fingers and bop our heads laced with fake hair, and are often seen as hostile and emasculating partners. To add to our woes, the fetishisation of black women has a long and deep history rooted in colonialism and slavery. Caren M. Holmes's essay 'The Colonial Roots of the Racial Fetishisation of Black Women' is a useful and short introduction to this topic.

She states that although women of all colours are 'reduced to sexual commodities by a patriarchal system', it is black women especially who find that their race, class and gender all contribute to their continued 'sexual debasement'.

> **I think people think they might look at me and be like, 'Oh yeah, I wanna bang her, but she would never be my girlfriend.' – Barbara**

University became the site where I was confronted with these issues head-on. When encountering students who had never spoken to a black girl, it was uncomfortable to think of all the preconceptions that existed before I even had a chance to open my mouth. I began to understand how desirability not only had a romantic dimension but also played a significant part in respectability politics, and how collapsed definitions of black women permeated every aspect of my university life. Widely believed stereotypes affected how we interacted with lecturers, tutors and also other students.

> **I think also a lot of people just didn't get that I was quite reserved. I feel like they expected me to be quite loud. – Kenya**

Through my own experiences and those of others in this book, it is clear that university is a trying time for most black girls and non-binary people when it comes to beauty, desirability and relationships. University can mean rejection, self-doubt and hopelessness. At the same time, it can also mean recognising your worth in its purest sense – not compromising for anyone and ultimately, knowing that there's nothing wrong with you, but something bigger with society.

## Season of Singleness

In my first year, while sitting in the corridor of my halls with my new neighbours, a white male student felt the need to tell us all that 'personally, I don't find black women attractive. That's just not my preference.' I wasn't shocked, or offended. But you could bet that I was angry. Before he could finish his sentence, I shot back, 'What makes you think black women would find you attractive anyway?' Don't get me wrong, the validation of men is not the be-all and end-all. What hit a nerve was his air of confidence and privilege, which screamed, 'I'm at the top of the food chain.' Comments like these serve to reinforce the obvious reality that women of colour, especially black women, are right at the bottom of society's heterosexual desirability hierarchy.

The conversation about beauty and desirability starts way before university. I have many fond memories of running around in my primary school playground, playing the game all children either love or hate: kiss chase. I was the fastest runner out of the boys and girls, so I usually did quite well. One lunchtime, however, it was the boys' turn to chase the girls. All of a sudden, I wasn't the fastest in the field any more. I ran around the playground, deliberately slowing down so I could be caught, ready to fake outrage at being kissed. Instead, I found that a number of the boys tactfully avoided me. Why didn't they catch me? I was right there! I soon realised that even if it meant shooting up in the ranks of kiss chase, there was no desire to kiss me.

It doesn't stop there. My experience at secondary school wasn't an anomaly. The dark-skinned black girls were always *too* dark, *too* loud or had *too* much of an attitude. Instead, 'lighties' and white girls were preferred. An all-girl group at my school of around ten to fifteen pupils were the perfect example of this – they nicknamed themselves 'The Slags', reclaiming the intended insult. They were the girls who hit puberty early, doused themselves in Victoria's Secret PINK mist, wore the most makeup and were exclusively white or light. To their full knowledge, all the boys loved them, and all the girls in school despised them. The Slags formed the blueprint for 'desirability' for those who wanted them and those who wanted to *be* them. No one was interested in darker-skinned girls, and that was clear.

**When I was in secondary school, I was always the ugly girl. People would call me 'gorilla', and it used to be so depressing because people would do their Facebook posts: 'Adaobi the Gorilla'. I internalised it around Year 9: I'm going to be ugly forever. – Adaobi**

I felt the same as Adaobi. If whiteness was the standard that all women were judged by, I was going to be ugly forever. My hair was never going to be straight, my nose was never going to be narrow and my skin was never going to be fair. So where could I go from there? At the same time, the very characteristics that most black women were and still are ridiculed for such as full lips, curves or a big bum were worshipped on whiter and lighter women. You only have to look at the 'blackfish-ing' debate, with white Instagram models accused of extreme tanning, dark make-up and hair braids, to see that the racially ambiguous look is 'in' right now.

I left for university adamant that I was not going to get into a relationship – but also convinced that no one was going to find me attractive anyway. It was a win-win situation, in a way. I used it as the basis to focus on myself, and not to *expect* anything when I got to uni-versity. I feel that most black girls go to university with this same mindset.

## Self-Love over Everything

Living in a world of edited images, algorithms and fake personalities, it becomes harder to believe that anyone truly loves themselves. I always believed that self-love was corny and embarrassing. What did it even mean? In my mind, it was an opportunity for those who extolled the message to write vague phrases like, 'You are worth it' or 'Love yourself', in pink, cursory calligraphy. Somehow the message was lost on me, and to an extent, still is.

To my surprise, going to university changed my understanding of self-love dramatically. University can be exciting for a number of reasons – one being that this will probably be your first time meeting such a wide range of new people. If you're like me, it will also be the time when you begin to realise the extent to which your personality, interests and likes have been defined by other people. I remember spending a lot of time in my first few months trying to work out who I was and most importantly, who I *wanted* to be. University is a fresh start.

Before anything, shatter your god complex and recognise that you are not perfect. In fact, you're very flawed. As black women, we often walk a fine line between false stereotypes or caricatures of the angry woman, the hypersexual woman, the flawless or magic 'Queen'. We are so used to working twice as hard for everything that neither failure nor having flaws is an option. We can't give anyone a reason to continue to deprive us of what we have worked hard for. This notion was detrimental to how I viewed myself – especially the idea that I wasn't *allowed* to have flaws. My actions at university would represent more than my own personal actions. There's a fear that your weaknesses and imperfections will be extrapolated as the prototype for all black students. Deconstructing this notion was refreshing, in that it reminded me that I'm a complex being, and one who makes mistakes.

**My self-image has improved, but there's still such a long way to go – but I think I'm now looking at myself . . . trying to appreciate the best parts of me instead of always voicing the worst parts of me. Because the person I was before is the kind of person that could not take a compliment. – Ayomide**

After you're done with your god complex, you will truly understand that comparison is self-love's arch-nemesis. With social media representations, we're under constant pressure to define where we are and what we are doing at all times. Progress is now understood and measured against what *others* are doing in their lives and how they're doing it. At university, the stark reality will hit home that you're now in an environment where you're likely to be surrounded by girls who are, in the eyes of society, the epitome of beauty and desirability.

**I used to say I wish[ed] I could be smaller, compact, petite, you know – more beautiful in the sense of adhering to those beauty standards. But then it just got to a point of, I back myself a hundred and ten per cent, I'm a good-looking girl, I don't need to look like this. – Renée**

In line with challenging this standard of beauty, I found it best to develop a healthy relationship with my natural hair. Hair texture and styles have an immense power and ability to shape our lives as black women. With some workplaces even describing afro hair and hairstyles as 'unprofessional', there is a racialised hierarchy embedded in the language of hair – one that feeds into respectability politics.

Having a healthy relationship with your hair doesn't necessarily mean joining the natural hair movement and putting flowers in it, but moving past seeing having your natural hair 'out' as a transitional stage to your next hairstyle. The relationship between black women and hair runs a lot deeper than just *hair*. It's often memories of sitting in between someone's legs and having your hair yanked with an afro comb, or in my case, being tapped on the back in assembly to be told the girl behind me couldn't see because my hair was too big.

For most of my first year, I refused to change my hair style too much because I wanted it to be 'consistent' – AKA, I didn't want people to ask me about my hair. So I kept it black, straight and long-bob length, and rarely went more than two days with it in its natural state. I truly believed that this would help me blend in as much as I could. With my race already a talking point, I didn't have the energy for my hair to be one also. With no natural hairdressers in Cambridge, my curly edges would be screaming for help by the end of term. But I always tried to maintain my straight style because I wasn't ready to have a conversation about why my hair looked different every two weeks.

**I remember when I had braids and I was nervous to change my hair – but I wanted to get a wig done, because it's easier. I remember just thinking, 'Oh, for fuck's sake, everyone's going to be talking about my hair tomorrow . . . it's going to be so long, I can't be bothered.' – Barbara**

**When I got braids . . . they'd be like, 'I love your dreadlocks' or, 'Wow, your hair grows so quickly.' – Eireann**

Hopefully, university is also a radical time – in that you see for yourself how flawed and narrow this conception of beauty is. There is no point in comparing yourself to something that is virtually impossible, and most importantly, isn't *you*. Be selfish and radical in choosing how to discover self-love, because you will be the only person to do it justice. Surround yourself with positive representations you can relate to both visually and academically. Read books, journals and articles on topics that interest you, and cushion yourself with validating information. At the same time, be careful not to attribute significance and importance to noise on the internet that lacks nuance. We are complex beings – 'complex' not meaning 'difficult', but deserving of the time it takes to work us out.

**The process of seeing myself as a desirable person only happened when I unlearned all the things that I was taught to learn throughout my life. So, desirability for me wasn't necessarily an external thing, I felt desirable once I desired myself. – Saredo**

Notice how many 'I's are in Saredo's statement? There has to be a point where your self-worth starts and stops with you. Especially during my first few weeks at Cambridge, I wanted everyone to have a positive perception of me. If that meant changing my character slightly depending on who I was with, then so be it. It was always me adapting to suit them in the hope of the highest honour: validation. Thankfully, I got over that very soon, once I realised that the people who genuinely knew me appreciated who I really was. (Or it might have been when my best friend's dad told me to stop speaking like I had a plum in my mouth.)

## Relationships at University

**I think it's a very natural urge at that time in your life to get straight into quite a serious relationship, because it's like you're rebuilding your own family and your support systems in a new space. – Micha**

The majority of black girls at university tended to look for relationships with people from the same racial or cultural background as them. There are very legitimate reasons why most of us choose to do this. You automatically assume – often rightly – that things will be a lot easier: same banter, same tastes, similar family backgrounds, all that good stuff. Most importantly, if there's a chance to skip the possibility of racism or fetishisation within your relationship – why not? With such a small number of black students in the overall university population, the potential pool of partners was always going to be small – so small that you had to check that your friend from ACS wasn't dating the same guy or girl. Can you imagine? A disaster waiting to happen. Oh, and the brutal truth was that most of the black boys just weren't interested in black girls at university. Everything society had told us so far about beauty, desirability and relationships didn't magically disappear; if anything, it was magnified tenfold.

No matter what we think, it seems that the external pressures from families and relatives also have an impact on how black girls view relationships at university. As Ọrẹ said in 'A Letter to my Fresher Self', many of us can relate to side-eyeing that one aunty who won't stop asking, 'When will you marry?' But can we really blame them? To our families on the outside, university is the perfect opportunity to find your potential partner, one who would have it all: a university degree, ambition, the prospect of a high-paying job. Of course, marriage and kids would shortly follow.

> **I was one of those people who before uni was like, *I'm coming to find my husband for sure*. Weren't we all? – Courtney**

Above all, our families love and want the best for us. In their eyes, it doesn't make sense that we are beautiful and smart, and yet cannot find anyone interested in us. Unsurprisingly, most black girls at university suddenly feel a sense of urgency. As a result, there is a strong sense of 'spouse-searching' at university, especially amongst those who choose to date exclusively within their own races. Going to universities with a tight-knit black community throws up plenty of opportunities to find black love – something that becomes even more important when your identity as a black student is politicised within predominately white institutions.

ACSs across the country host 'ACS Take Me Out' in a bid to pair up ACS members. This is based on the popular TV show *Take Me Out*, where contestants are on the lookout for one lucky girl to take to the Isle of Fernando's! Due to budgeting issues, our ACS committee could only afford to sponsor a trip to Nando's in the centre of town (see what we did there?). At UCL, the dress code for their version of ACS Take Me Out was 'Melanin Popping, Bae-merising Excellence'. I'm not sure how you dress up to be 'Bae-merising Excellence', but I respect it.

In first year, Ọrẹ and I went to our first ever ACS Take Me Out. Cambridge ACS had paired up with Anglia Ruskin's ACS because Cambridge had barely enough black people to be able to run consistently well-attended events. Ọrẹ and I were both picked to be one of the girls who popped their balloons when they weren't interested in a boy. From the beginning, Ọrẹ had her eyes on this tall, funny and very handsome guy from Cambridge. Did I mention he was a medic as well? Yeah. Anyway, she pulled me to the side to tell me that no matter how appealing this guy was to me, I had to pop my balloon and then she could get the date. I had just started seeing my boyfriend, which no one knew about yet, so this worked perfectly for me because I needed an out. Later, I watched her strut past the crowds in her black boob-tube dress and strappy heels, hand-in-hand with the medic as they walked out of the room to organise their date. Picture me beaming in the background like a proud mum on her wedding day.

As you can imagine, ACS Take Me Outs are a lot of fun, and a great sense of validation for heterosexual black women who are often left at the bottom when it comes to university dating.

**Because people come to ACS looking for a partner, they come like, 'I've got three years! I need to find someone. I NEED TO GRAFT!'**
**– Barbara**

Funnily enough, Barbara met her current boyfriend through ACS when she least expected it. They had both applied to be on the committee for ACS, and got to know each other more through the society. In many ways, people viewed their union as sacred because of how little we see strong representations of black love. In Barbara's own words, 'It's like, "**Oh my gosh, two black medics, oh my gosh, your kids**."' But she did mention that at the beginning it was hard because everyone wanted to know what was going on. When would they make it official? Were they arguing or fighting? Would it last? The tight-knit nature of the community of black students at university can sometimes be suffocating. It's like being in a large friendship group with dozens of off-shoot branches. You only have to tell a couple of people your business before everyone knows.

The dating scene and relationships also differ for black LGBTQ+ students. Almost all universities have their own LGBTQ+ societies, which can be a great way to meet new queer people and find a community. Bristol University's LGBTQ+ society hosts a BME mingle for freshers as an opportunity to meet other BME LGBTQ+ people. Or take FUSE Cambridge, for example, the network for LGBTQ+ people of colour, where students can attend socials and group movie nights to watch films or documentaries like *Moonlight* and *Tongues United*. It's an opportunity to become active within the queer community at Cambridge. Both are just some of the important spaces that allow BME LGBTQ+ people to safely express all overlapping aspects of their identity.

**I prefer the queer community and it's a space I like to surround myself with, so I inevitably end up dating more women and non-binary people. – Saskia**

So often, the stories of black LGBTQ+ students have been written out of the wider 'black experience' at university. The experiences of black LGBTQ+ students are often ones of navigating an environment that seeks to dehumanise your identity on both racial and sexual fronts. Stonewall's 'LGBT in Britain's Universities' Report asked 522 LGBT students about their experiences, highlighting what may be to some startling results. More than two in five LGBT students (42 per cent) hid or disguised the fact that they were LGBT at university due to fears of discrimination. Similarly, one in four non-binary students (24 per cent) and one in six trans students (16 per cent) didn't feel that they were able to wear clothes which offered a true reflection of their gender expression.

When we talk about 'black students', who do we mean? There is little to no discussion of black LGBTQ+ students, who are often faced with straddling multiple identities, rejecting one to accommodate another. Also, hardly spoken about or addressed is the rife homophobia, transphobia and biphobia within black communities, and specifically ACSs. The University of Oxford's 'Trans Report' in 2018 recognised that the 'transphobia experienced by trans people of colour is often racialised'. Prevailing notions of family, collective unity and the role of religion continue to have a large influence on most of our values today. Black LGBTQ+ students face the constant possibility of cultural estrangement from other black students within their own universities. Societies such as ACS can become stomping grounds for projecting a particular type of 'blackness', one that prioritises heterosexual black students.

The reality is that for anyone, sustaining a relationship at university is difficult and can be a pretty big commitment. They require time, sacrifice and, in most cases, selflessness on both ends if you really want the relationship to stand the test. It can be nice, though, to have someone at university who is specifically looking out for you backing your corner. It also relieved a lot of stress to have someone to binge-watch *House of Cards* and *How To Get Away With Murder* with after a long day. Just saying.

### Interracial Dating at University

The first conversation I ever had with my now-boyfriend, Joe, was at a 90s-themed bop. Bops, Cambridge's equivalent of school discos, can be *very* interesting affairs. They're usually themed, play exclusively cheesy music, are stocked with VK Vodka Kicks, and are attended by almost everyone in college. At my college, bops were banned – much to the disappointment of many students – for the majority of my second year after wee, vomit and poo were found scattered across college grounds.

Needless to say, I wasn't looking forward to my first bop. I was probably most annoyed that the people on my corridor had actually convinced me to leave my room in a 90s bomber jacket and neon leg warmers. As expected, the bop was one of the worst things that I had ever experienced – but luckily Joe felt the same. He tapped me on the shoulder and asked if I wanted to join him outside for some fresh air. A bit confused, I agreed, and we sat on the stone step outside our accommodation block. We spoke about a lot of things that night: our families, where we grew up, what our favourite colours were and what we expected from Cambridge.

Now is a good time to mention that Joe is a white British boy, and this whole interaction came to me as a surprise. Growing up around Essex, attending a pre-dominately white school, I believed it to be a fact that both white *and* black boys did not find black girls attractive. I remember feeling tense and listing all of the other reasons why Joe might *want* to talk to me, but most of all I was worried that he would say some of the things that I had heard before. 'If you were a chocolate you would be Galaxy'; 'I like you because you're a coconut: black on the outside, white on the inside'; or 'You're different to *other* black girls.' I knew that university was supposed to be a time to experience and to explore. Maybe I, being a black girl, would be part of that 'experience' package. I promised myself that at any slight hint of 'Swirl YouTube', where interracial couples document their relationships, I'd be out.

For some, interracial relationships have become a lucrative lifestyle. Think Jamie and Nikki, an Australian couple with over 1.7 million YouTube subscribers, or HelloBianca, a channel amassing 55,000 subscribers. Maybe they're just living their lives, but it's really hard to ignore the obsession of their fans, who like to see black and white uniting as a sign that racism is well and truly over.

**I've internalised to not even bother paying attention to white guys if you're looking at them romantically. Because in my head it was, *white guys are never going to like you*. – Ọrẹ**

**How do we, now that we're educated on institutional racism and oppressive structures, navigate something that is more emotionally based but still has that element pervasive within it? – Renée**

Being in an interracial relationship isn't a pass to overlook the wider structures that politicise these very relationships, though.

**When I was in a relationship with him, I was very clear that my blackness is not up for debate. – Fope**

Fast-forward almost four years: Joe and I are still together, and in a relationship that prioritises conversations about race, not one that sweeps them under the carpet and pretends that we inhabit a post-racial society. Race colours the very fabric of everything we do, and it would be irresponsible to ignore that. But most importantly, I managed to find someone that I love, who respects my experiences, makes me belly-laugh and is committed to, in his own words, 'helping you live your best life'.

However, it wasn't all plain sailing and heart-shaped chocolates. I had a few black male students feel they could self-righteously comment on my relationship and what I should be doing. Often in all-black settings

I was told I didn't give any of the other black boys 'a chance' given that I got together with my boyfriend in my first year. There was a worrying sense of entitlement over my choices, but most of all I felt disrespected.

The sense of betrayal eroded the strong solidarity that is espoused between black students within predominately white institutions. Interracial relationships are complicated enough, but I found this factor complicated it even further. It became hard for others to accept the fact that I had just happened to find someone I really liked. I soon learnt that I wasn't obliged to jump through hoops to explain it to anyone, or bash anyone in the process of doing so. But it was frustrating that I didn't have the privilege of being in a regular relationship, where no one cared what we did and how we did it. Our relationship was collapsed into black and white – quite literally.

*

For the tough-skinned, it's easy to ignore the elephant in the room that is racism when it comes to interracial relationships. At university, it became hard to gloss over the blatant fetishisation of black men at predominately white institutions, from idolising their physical bodies and stature in a sporting context, to relationships and sex. For most black men, it is an uncomfortable reality that their bodies are commodified to the point that they are always expected to perform a certain standard of 'black masculinity'. Even more so, the masculine expectations are particularly hard to grapple with for black queer men or gender non-conforming people who may want to present or date in a way that doesn't necessarily meet a heterosexual standard. As such, many black queer men have found their experiences and existence simultaneously defined and erased by racism.

Yet it is no secret that black male students have a 'unique' appeal to women and men of all races and ethnicities and have the opportunity to capitalise on that. Among all those Ọrẹ and I interviewed, there was a collective sense of agreement that a select few black men at university simply didn't mind that most people were attracted to them – albeit some for the wrong reasons.

**I think it also comes down to black men having a market, or a lot of choice – because they could still get with white girls very easily because of that fetishisation or that exploration of that interracial interaction. – Courtney**

**I think the worst thing is when I have a crush on someone but – am I even his type? In terms of: is 'black girls' his type? Which I think a lot of white women just have never ever had to think about. – Fope**

Heterosexual black male privilege is well discussed in black feminist circles. There has never been a denial of the racism and unique prejudice that black men face, but a critical analysis of the contours of their privilege in relation to the experiences of black women is necessary. Within university walls, engaging in patriarchal rituals such as sports-related heavy drinking allows most black men to very conveniently buy into 'lad culture' and slip into 'cool' stereotypes.

When a black male student was pursued by a non-black woman, it was more likely to be deemed a sense of validation and acceptance – and a welcome one for some black male students, who were just trying to get by 'quietly' at university and blend in as much as possible. Many heterosexual black men were complicit in ignoring this issue, and chose to disengage. They didn't want to acknowledge that there was yet *another* thing that black students needed to be wary of. Any whiff of fetishisation was usually dismissed, in order to avoid 'unnecessary fuss'. In some cases, it was even spun into the age-old and tired story of black women feeling bitter or upset that black men were desired by non-black individuals. One black male student at my university even said that we black girls shouldn't be upset that he wasn't dating 'one of us' (for the record, no one was actually upset).

**The class and prestige to get in with the white people carries on throughout society. Once you get to a certain level, you want to show that actually your whole life reflects that level, including your personal relationships. – Adaobi**

The very same interactions became validation tools for non-black students, who almost obsessively insisted that they were 'not racist' because they found black men attractive. In an article titled 'I'm not an object or a toy for your white gaze – don't fetishise me as a black man', Archie Mustow, a recent law graduate, explored what it was like to date as a black man:

**It's almost as if white people feel guilty that they get to be white and I have to be black, so they take on the noble role of reminding me that there are some benefits to my negroness by being my mate or wanting to have sex with me.**

Lazing around on the grass one day, one of my favourite friends told me that he had been invited to an exclusive dinner at an all-girls college where each girl had been tasked to bring one boy with them. He told me that at the dinner most of the girls, all white, joked about *reserving* him and his brothers to have babies with. 'Our babies would be *so* cute,' they said.

I did a workshop for the [day] talking about online dating, and a lot of my group in the morning were white people. I was explaining that your preferences can be racist, and one girl was like, 'It's not my fault I like black guys because I like broad noses and flat foreheads.' I was like, 'You've just described Vin Diesel.' – Fope

When I've spoken to black guys about it . . . they've said that the black girls are the ones that they settle with after they're done having their fun. – Kenya

You think your black queen will just be waiting for you while you're doing your rubbish in university? – Renée

And that is it, isn't it? Kenya and Renée have said what a lot of us were thinking. It was known among black men at university that most black girls had little to no choice in a tiny pool of potential partners. Some black men exploited this fact, knowing that a few of us had no option but to wait around. But as I mentioned above, when I decided I was not going to entertain the idea of 'waiting around', I was suddenly treated like a traitor – despite black men having the agency and sexual freedom to have relationships with anyone.

**I love black men, and I know I love black men, but I think that loving black men is a very painful process, because a lot of the time that kind of love is unrequited. Not just in a romantic sense, but I feel like I spend a lot of my time making sure that I'm being supportive to black men who don't put in the same kind of work to support me in return. – Ọrẹ**

We saw how some black men acted at university, and for most of us, it was hurtful. That hurt wasn't only because they weren't interested – I truly believe that is something that shouldn't be forced. But most of them had failed to realise that by their internalising and accepting of racialised notions of desirability, us black women were affected very strongly. It was a reminder that interracial relationships and the structures of power around them are still contentious, and as always, vitally important to deconstruct.

## Reclaiming Bodies

I think it's fair to say that you will often find the words 'university' and 'sex' in the same sentence. For most, university is an exciting time that allows for the agency to explore sexual relationships. Or perhaps, everything feels new and distant because of the lack of sex education. In my first sex education class in Year 6, one of my classmates ran out of the room straight to the toilets to be sick after watching our teacher awkwardly put a condom on a banana. Since that point, I have never been 'educated' on matters regarding sex, relationships or sexual assault. They all seemed to be things that you had to *experience* to really understand. Even now, when we watch sex scenes on TV, listen to relationship 'experts' and seek advice from our friends, their realities will never quite match our own.

A survey conducted by Hexjam looked at the sex lives of around 5,800 students up and down the UK, and revealed that around 25 per cent of students lost their virginity at university. This merely confirms what we all know: university is a prime time to explore sex and sexualities. Student unions across the country are prepped for the wave of excited freshers, issuing thousands of free condoms and pregnancy tests. All of a sudden, you're thrust into a world where the pressure to have sex is immense. You feel as if this is all everyone is

205

doing all the time, and they all want someone to talk to about it – you know, the typical, 'I had to do the walk of shame last night' that forces you to ask all about your friend's antics.

> **People just used to sleep around, and everyone is speaking to each other or like seeing each other, but no one's actually putting any goddamn labels on it, and I'm not here for that . . . The mixed messages, ugh: it's just annoying. – Nathania**

A key component of my freshers' week was a compulsory session on consent, part of a long series of introductory talks about what college life would be like, and how to exit a building on fire. The session included a video called 'Tea and Consent', which compared sexual consent to making someone a cup a tea. 'If they say, "No, thank you,"' the narrator explained, 'then don't make them tea. *At all.*' Most of the people in the room laughed nervously. It seemed like such a gross oversimplification that it left most of us wondering how anyone could possibly *not* understand it?

'The body is an appropriate cultural symbol to explore the links between colonialism and patriarchal capitalism,' says Dr Akeia Benard, a professor from Wheelock College, Boston – meaning for black women, the conversation regarding sexual assault and harassment is particularly worrying when considering the historical trajectory of sexual violence and exploitation against black bodies. In my second year at university, I will never forget how the historian of racial and sexual violence Danielle L. McGuire detailed the case of Betty Jean Owens, an African American woman brutally raped by four white men in Tallahassee, Florida in 1959. Students mobilised for her cause when the student leader Buford Gibson 'universalised the attack', stating that 'you must remember it wasn't just one Negro girl that was raped, it was all of Negro womanhood in the South'. The exploitation of black women's bodies served as a reminder of white supremacy and a signpost of a social order that would continue to control black women's bodies.

Recently, we've seen the rise of the #MeToo movement, an online campaign supporting the survivors of sexual assault, abuse and harassment. The movement has reverberated across the globe, being joined by other hashtags such as #balancetonporc and #yotambien. #MeToo conjures images of glitzy Hollywood stars who defiantly wore all-black at the 2018 Golden Globes – with little consideration given to Tarana Burke, the black woman who launched the movement almost a decade ago. Burke told ESSENCE magazine, 'The world responds to the vulnerability of white women.

Our narrative has never been centred in mainstream media. Our stories don't get told and as a result, it makes us feel not as valuable.'

Every person Ọrẹ and I interviewed had been, or at least knew one other person who had been, sexually assaulted whilst at university. For those who don't understand or doubt the severity of sexual assault at university:

- 62 per cent of students and graduates have experienced sexual violence.

- Only 2 per cent of those experiencing sexual violence felt able to report it to their university and were satisfied with their university's reporting process.

- 33 per cent have no knowledge or very little knowledge about where to seek support if they experience sexual violence.

**I think the right question would be: who *hasn't* been a victim? – Mikai**

Universities across the UK have become grounds for assault, harassment and misconduct. This is a crisis affecting not only students, but also staff. It's not a new phenomenon to many of us, who are familiar with having to navigate conversations in fear of being blamed or further silenced. The conversation and language surrounding sexual assault and harassment continues to be part of a broader culture of victim blaming. Women are asked whether or not we were drunk, or what we were wearing, as a means of 'contextualising' sexual assault or harassment. It's as if the severity of the disciplinary procedure (or worse) is determined by whether or not the crime was in some way the victim's 'fault'.

This has widened the scope and range of what both students and staff deem to be sexual assault or harassment. In particular, lad culture, and its connection to social and educational privileges, has dramatically influenced the university environment. The NUS project 'That's What She Said' found that most students defined lad culture as 'a group or "pack" mentality residing in activities such as sport and heavy alcohol consumption, and "banter" which was often sexist, misogynist, and homophobic', and I would add, racist. With lad culture having such an influence on the social aspects of university, little effort is made to address the underlying cultural element of sexual abuse. Instead, most universities continue to address each report as it comes, rather than understanding how it fits into a wider and urgent conversation regarding university culture, sexual harassment and sexual violence. It is clear most universities are still not ready to address how this issue is embedded, rooted and perpetuated by the culture.

Men are often excused with the saying, 'boys will be boys', or 'just having a laugh'. Especially within the campus environment, sexual abuse and violence have been institutionally accepted and trivialised. In 2018, a group of eleven male students from the University of Warwick were revealed to have set up a group chat discussion in which they talked about raping and sexually assaulting other students. Comments included, 'Sometimes it's fun to just go wild and rape 100 girls', whilst one mentioned, 'Even the pakis??', and another 'I cannot wait to have surprise sex with some freshers.' In total, ninety-eight screenshots from the chat were sent to the University of Warwick as part of the complaint – enough, you would think, for the university to take appropriate action against the students? Well, no.

First of all, the university's director of press was appointed as the official investigator, a clear conflict of interests. Secondly, Vice-Chancellor Professor Stuart Croft wrote an open letter in which he spent two paragraphs detailing his 'shock', before setting out what the next steps would be. He went on to explain that 'we have a duty of care to all involved, as they are our students' and that the students involved will bear the brunt of the incident 'forward on their cvs [sic]'. Two of the men involved in the group chat would have an initial ten-year campus ban reduced to one. And still no mention of the students affected or their wellbeing, nor of the justification for such lenient disciplinary processes. Instead, there was an insistence on arbitrary terms such as 'the law', 'the courts' and 'justice'.

The university was apparently eager to put forward the notion that these students were an 'exceptional case' or 'bad apples'. Warwick students were not so easily placated, however. By 5 p.m. the next day, after an instant and sizeable backlash, the university performed an abrupt U-turn, and announced that two of the students would not be returning to Warwick at all. Its institutional culture was left unexamined, unchallenged and intact; it was only a media storm that forced it to change its position.

In 1994, the Zellick Report was published, an important guidance document regarding student disciplinary procedures such as the one at Warwick. The report suggested that universities should *not* take internal disciplinary action when it came to alleged misconduct. This has allowed universities to inadequately address a myriad of events that accompany sexual violence: disciplinary procedures, specialist aftercare and, most importantly, rebuilding the trust of students. Some of you may be surprised to find out that most universities still follow these very guidelines. This correlates with the sheer amount of sexual violence that goes unreported at universities. Compounded with sub-standard university regulations surrounding issues of sexual assault, it begs the question of how universities have managed to get away with being complicit in this manner.

As a result students, particularly women, feel unsupported, dismissed and disconnected from their universities. As That's What She Said rightly states, 'the growing individualism which is an aspect of corporate higher education may also prevent students, female and male, from reaching out for help when they experience difficulties'. Despite being published in 2013, the report still resonates today. As students, we often feel that our everyday issues and trials are miniscule in comparison to the bigger elements of university business, such as competition and privatisation. We're rarely seen as human beings with individual needs that are specific and complex, but rather as paying customers, existing within the university only for a short period.

Above all, it has taken generations of tireless women's officers and student activists on the ground to urge universities and, in some cases, to work with universities, to address this endemic crisis. When someone is a victim of sexual violence it reverberates across the student body. For every initiative, policy and campaign, it is clear that the main driving force is always from students.

Every year, University Student Unions organise a march entitled 'Reclaim the Night'. Reclaim the Night started in 1977 across England in Leeds, York, Bristol, Manchester and other cities. The Leeds Revolutionary Feminist group wanted to take collective action regarding male sexual violence against women, and to honour the histories of those who have come before us and the challenges they have faced throughout history. Manchester Student Union have rallied around the Night to encourage students to volunteer, write to the local council and sign a petition addressed to Manchester City Council to 'Make our Streets Safer'.

Reclaim the Night, amongst other ongoing campaigns by students, has contributed to a growing pressure on universities to admit responsibility. 'Where do you draw the line?' is a harassment prevention approach developed by UCL, Oxford, Cambridge and Manchester, all of which recognise that harassment within academia tends to be more nuanced and covert. Similarly, Cambridge's new 'zero tolerance' stance on harassment and abuse is conveyed in its 'Breaking The Silence' campaign. The university now has an anonymous reporting system embedded in its website, allowing any member of the university to report and record misconduct. However, this all comes only after women and non-binary students have worked to create spaces for themselves and for victims of sexual assault. Such actions have paved the way for the creation of standardised and comprehensive guidelines for alleged misconduct which prioritise victims/survivors first, rather than the reputations of institutions.

Under no circumstances is there an excuse for sexual violence. As stated by Rape Crisis, '100% of the responsibility for any act of sexual violence lies with the perpetrator'. As such, if you have ever been a victim, suspect you have been a victim or know someone who is a victim, where possible seek professional help from a professional organisation. Contact the Rape Crisis national freephone helpline on 0808 802 9999, or the National Domestic Violence Helpline on 0808 2000 247, or ring NHS 111. It's daunting and uncomfortable, but there are professionals out there who are trained, experienced and willing to help.

You may find yourself in a position where a friend or somebody close discloses to you that they have been a victim of sexual violence. First of all, it's important that you let them know that you care and that you believe what they are telling you. Despite the vilification of sexual assault victims in the media, it is *very* unlikely that someone will be lying about their experience of any form of sexual violence. It's about trust and allowing them to tell their own story when it is best for them. It could also be an idea to familiarise yourself with your university's disciplinary procedure and what steps your friend might want to take if they choose to do so. But above all, look after yourself and your needs. By all means you can be a supportive shoulder, but trust your friend to make the right decisions.

At the back of this book, you can find a small but useful directory of resources relating to sexual assault – for victims and supporters. From sharpening up your own understanding of consent and accessing helplines to supporting and organising, this can be a place to turn to if you're not sure where to start.

## Choosing You

Getting to a stage of self-worth and self-love can be difficult and tiresome. It's easy to understand from all the above why we're more likely to experience feelings of self-hate and inadequacy. You're trying to be your best self – trying to be the most successful and empowered version of yourself – only to realise that it doesn't quite fit into this whole scale of desirability, palatability and subservience that women, especially black women, are often expected to adhere to.

If you take away anything from this chapter, let it be this: try to be kinder to yourself. *Please.* We are our own worst critics, and sometimes we need to cut ourselves some slack. It's about setting boundaries and practising good self-care – both acts which will put you first. Even though it sounds so simple, this strategy was revolutionary for me at university.

Taking a whistle-stop tour through everyone's university experiences was enough to witness the growth and constant learning curve that is involved in learning to love yourself with no excuses. It takes time, and there's no set blueprint for 'how to do it'. Don't expect to come into a university environment knowing everything.

Instead, you will grow, and you will learn. In my humble opinion, that's the best part about it.

Oh, and feel free to tell that one aunty all of this. I'm sure she'll understand!

# 6

## *Blacktivism*

### Ọrẹ

It was November 2015, my first term at Cambridge, and I had just got back from my first ACS event. I shared a cab with Amatey Doku, who was then the president of Jesus College's student union. As one of the few black students at Cambridge in an elected office, he was someone I looked up to from very early on in my time there. We were heading back to our rooms, and our saying goodbyes turned into an hour-long conversation about a whole range of things. I knew that his tenure as president would end that December, so I asked him what he was going to do afterwards. Then he told me about the cockerel. There was a bronze cockerel that sat in our college hall which had been taken during the 1897 Benin Expedition and bequeathed to the university by George William Neville. All of this was written on a plaque beneath the cockerel – in Latin, of course, because we know Cambridge loves some good old Latin!

I remember feeling shocked that this cockerel had been there and I hadn't noticed it. More shocking, though, was knowing that it was being displayed as if it were a trophy to be proud of, despite the knowledge of its history. The college couldn't feign ignorance about the circumstances surrounding when or how the artefact was acquired because they had engraved it on the plaque right below. The 1897 Benin Expedition was a British-led military expedition that became a pretext for the colonial occupation of what was once one of the most powerful West African kingdoms, the Benin Empire. The retaliatory expedition was intentionally meant to obliterate the Empire, and after burning and destroying the city, the British army looted the artefacts left in its wake, which are now held in museums and institutions across the Western world.

Amatey told me that once his presidency was over, he wanted to work to get the cockerel taken down and repatriated to Benin City (in modern-day Nigeria). As a Nigerian myself, I felt an obligation to get on board. If we couldn't fight for this, who would? Amatey made it sound so simple. We would write a proposal and spell out the already blatantly obvious injustice that was this cockerel's possession. There would be huge uproar, and it would be back in Benin in no time.

Little had we considered how much resistance we would encounter. Obviously, we were going up against an age-old institution, built, in certain respects, on imperialist legacies, and stuck in its traditional ways. We sought approval from the college student body to strengthen our case. We had to wait until the next Ordinary General Meeting (OGM) to raise a motion, present our proposal and then have the student body vote on it. Our team grew, and we worked on a proposal that outlined that keeping the cockerel was immoral in itself, particularly given how it made students from former colonies feel, and also that repatriation might turn out to be beneficial for the college. We added the second point because Amatey and I felt that a moral incentive alone wasn't enough, and that we had to negotiate with the college by showing them what was in it for them. This point in particular became a grave source of conflict within our team, and the night before the OGM, two people resigned from the group.

We thought that our biggest opposition would be from a few ignorant white students or empire nostalgics who were more concerned with the monetary value of the cockerel than with the history of its acquisition – but that wasn't the case. Instead, we faced opposition from

221

a group of BME students who thought that we were stressing the material incentives for the college when actually the only reason that the college should have needed to repatriate the cockerel was moral. As far as they were concerned, it was stolen, so it should be returned. I do not entirely disagree – but as a first-year student, I was afraid of being seen as a troublemaker, and felt that I could be putting my place at Cambridge on the line. So I opted for what I thought would be the path of least resistance.

I learnt the hard way that just because people look like you or have comparable experiences with oppression doesn't mean that they will be on your side. We might all be minorities and we might all be engaged with activism, fighting to validate our voices in these oppressive circumstances, but we aren't a monolith. One of our members who had resigned showed up at the OGM, dressed as a Black Panther, with a whole team of friends who were also dressed all in black. The OGM turned into a mini-warzone.

As we were to discover, when you fight for things you believe in, you will make enemies. You expect enemies to be vicious, but when your friends turn on you, it takes on a different meaning. That's a pain that no one prepared me for. Attacks were made on my character. Having spent most of the meeting trying not to cry, when I couldn't hold it in any more, I wept.

After the two-hour-long OGM and a few days of team meetings, during which we revised the proposal, we presented a modified, extended proposal to the college. We were invited to meet with numerous college committees we had never heard of; the longer the process went on, the more unclear it became as to whether or not the college was actually going to do anything at all. Attempting to make any change at universities like Cambridge that are so stubbornly attached to 'tradition' takes forever. I think the expectation from the authorities was that we would be wearied by the wait, and that our fatigue would work in their favour.

We had to sit in lots of meetings with university officials who challenged our position that the plights of the Benin people, who had been requesting for over a century that their art be repatriated, were valid. They would ask questions like, 'But who's going to look after it?', as if the people from whom it was stolen hadn't been doing so perfectly well for centuries. Our well-researched responses never appeased them.

And that's how that story ended. (Or perhaps it hasn't ended yet.) After years of meetings, the cockerel has still not made it back to Benin in Nigeria, and neither the college nor the university ever gave us a reason as to why. Although it was taken down from the hall and the shelf removed, so we could be sure it wasn't going back up, we still have no clue where it has been kept.

However, my work on this campaign was not entirely fruitless. I raised considerable awareness about an underdiscussed issue that's very close to my heart as a Nigerian, and I set a ball in motion. It was a very steep learning curve for me. This was my first dip into Cambridge's 'activism' space, it was painful and tiring, and still we have not got the results that we wanted.

Fight the good fight – but be prepared for the difficult, less glamorous bits. Fighting for issues that affect people like us in white-dominated spaces will always be an uphill battle, but if we don't do it, who will? I had to constantly remind myself about the generation of black students who would come after me and never have to shudder at the sight of colonial war loot being celebrated in their dining hall.

We had to make our case in rooms full of white people who will never know what it is like to be black in an institution that seems to take pride in its ties with an imperialist history. And we had to make our case again, and again, and again, as everyone shifted in their shoes trying to decide who to pass us on to, so that they didn't have to be the ones to say no.

**That's how they get away with stuff: institutional memory. Because everyone is here for like three years, then they leave – so any big issue, if you just wait long enough, it will be dead. – Arenike**

Like most black girls at university, I didn't go in with a plan to engage in as much activism or political work as I did. But as a black woman in a white dominated space, I discovered that my very existence was an act of resistance. Although I wasn't looking for it, the political work found me.

## The Burden of Obligation

Regardless of how hard it was and how fruitless it sometimes felt, I'm glad that I decided to get involved with the Benin Bronze repatriation campaign. Simply put, I made the initial decision to help because I felt like I *had to*; I felt obliged by my very identity as a Nigerian woman to do something. Since I had been given this privilege of being at such a renowned institution, the very least I could do was fight for every issue that concerned people like me, especially those who weren't there to fight their cases. I'm a black, Nigerian-British woman, and I realise that 'people like me' encompasses a significant percentage of the population.

As black girls, the activist instinct is bound up in our very identities. The more aware we become of our own oppression, the more we feel the need to fight for every cause. We have to stand up for black women and battle the insidious misogynoir we face, because other black women fought before us in order for us to be there. We have to fight for all women too, challenging gender-based violence and diversifying white feminist spaces while we're at it. Then we have to fight for the whole black community – even black men who, though they can be part of the problem, are still affected by racism in a unique way. Then we learn about the importance of intersectionality and the extent to which all the axes of oppression are mutually reinforcing and suddenly, we are carrying the plights of the whole world on our backs. Suddenly, we feel an obligation to fight everyone's corner. Suddenly, we are haunted by guilt if we do not.

To understand why the black experience is unique, it's important to examine why *we* feel the obligation to be politically active and engage in the ongoing fight for black progress, while our white counterparts have the privilege of choosing to jog on, oblivious to the realities of racism around them. Some white people may not be bothered; others may be afraid; but even those who do choose to man the trenches with us still have the privilege of choosing to ignore racism if they want to. When it's inextricably bound to every part of your life, as it is for black students, you don't.

**To what extent are black students not privileged with mediocrity? Why must we feel the need, why are we obligated to make a difference? Why are we obligated to make an impact? – Renée**

It's not merely an obligation that we feel within, it is an obligation that is placed on us. We're assumed to be the founts of all knowledge on everything concerning blackness, and to have an opinion on everything that affects black people everywhere. But what if you don't?

What if sometimes you just want to focus on your degree, and graduate? What if you just want to pursue other interests?

I had a really insightful conversation with Adaobi about how it is always assumed that the purpose of absolutely everything we do as black women is for the betterment of black people. Adaobi is very passionate about robotics, and has struggled with the fact that the white men she encounters in the tech world assume that her primary reason for entering the industry is to solve its very pertinent diversity problem.

**I really am for black women, but I came here to be the CEO or the Team Lead – so why do I need to be the Diversity and Inclusion Officer? People think that all I do is driven by diversity and my life is no longer my own, my interests are no longer my own. I can't do something just because I enjoy it. – Adaobi**

The pressure of feeling as if you're obliged to constantly fight for your people can become a burden. Not everyone wants to be, or has to be, a community leader or a spokesperson in activist spaces. Try not to feel guilty for being passionate about things other than diversity quotas. Be an Adaobi and reclaim ownership over your interests.

Your interests may not be the only reason you choose to disengage with political work. The stress and fatigue can be a lot to manage alongside your studies. In my first year I chose the Benin Bronze campaign, and in my second and third years I focused on the ACS's access work. By the time our lecturers went on strike in the second term of my final year, following a drastic cut in their pensions, I was tired. By the time the Decolonise the Curriculum movement was picking up steam, with alternative reading lists being drafted and focus groups making real headway with department officials on diversifying the curriculum, I was exhausted. Regardless, people expected me, in my most stressful year at Cambridge, to keep showing up, and to have an opinion, and to be actively involved. I didn't know how to explain the fatigue without feeling bad for not being there to fight for a cause that might need me.

Fope can relate:

**When someone knows you for always putting your opinion forward, being very bold with that, especially in political spaces, people tend to then ask you to do more and more and more. It's always, 'You know what, Fope will call this out, so I'll ask Fope to do this,' or 'Fope should go for this role because Fope would be really good at**

**it.' It's not taken into account that Fope has a
life. Fope has very, very little energy to expend.**

Learning to say no to this 'obligation' is difficult. Not
only are we always expected to fight, it is assumed that
all we care about is fighting, and that we will always
want to fight. But sometimes, we want to rest and
recover and focus on staying sane in what is already a
troubling environment.

By my third year, I wasn't just physically and mentally
tired of the struggle, I was also emotionally drained.
The more engaged you try to be, the more aware you
become of exactly how oppressed you are. I hate the
way the word 'woke' is thrown around, but I appreciate
how it helps us to conceptualise what it feels like to
come to *see* your oppression. The awakening is painful
and distressing. Every time you engage in the kind of
activism that feels personal and proximal, you relive
the anger, the frustration, and the helplessness of fighting a system of oppression so deeply entrenched that it's
difficult to know where to begin. For some people, this
pain is enough to dissuade them from doing any activism at all. But for those of us whose instinct to act is too
strong to push back, remember that it's okay to stop,
recover and look after yourself.

**The power in solidarity can be very, very intoxicating, and you want to do everything, but you're going to burn out. – Fope**

Choosing to opt out of political work and say no to student movements that might need you is not just self-care but also self-preservation. It's not everyday politics – sometimes rest, beloved. Rest.

### The B in B(A)ME

This burden of obligation is something that BME (or BAME – black, Asian and minority ethnic) students feel especially. BME isn't a term that I had encountered before university, but much to the annoyance of almost everyone we interviewed for this book, it is often at the centre of these 'diversity' discussions. It's difficult to pinpoint when it became popularised. Some say it developed out of the notion of 'political blackness' used in British anti-racism movements in the 1970s. However, some suggest it didn't become used officially until the early 1990s, when the UK census categories used 'ethnic minority' to refer to everyone non-white. If you find yourself in political spaces, more often than not, you will be grouped under BME, or 'people of colour'.

The term BME is unhelpful. The idea of black *and* minority ethnic firstly implies that black is not an ethnic minority – but for now, that is beside the point. No one we spoke to had anything positive to say about the term.

**Don't call me woman of colour. Don't call me BME. – Adaobi**

**Throw it in the bin or something. Bin it. – Mikai**

The term is problematic because it lacks nuance. It conflates all non-white people, and treats them as a monolith. Yet our experiences of race and racism as people of colour are very different. The term speaks to the idea of white normativity – that every other race is constructed as deviant from whiteness, as 'lacking' in whiteness. The idea of political blackness has a similar effect. Eireann says, '**No group is in direct opposition to whiteness,**' but terms like BME and 'politically black' suggest that this is in fact the case.

> **I feel like black people are at the bottom of the totem pole and I don't feel like our issues are comparable to [other] racial groups. – Kenya**

> **I think at Cambridge specifically, black people face specific resistances and hostilities from the institution that I don't think can be applied to, let's say, Pakistani or Chinese international students. – Chelsea**

The term BME prevents us from having frank conversations about the unique ways in which black people in particular experience racism. It silences. Even in writing this book, I felt an initial need to apologise for not speaking directly to all women of colour – but why should I? Without trying to engage in 'oppression Olympics' here, when Kenya spoke about being at the bottom of the totem pole, it resonated with me. Even though we might all be bracketed under BME in research papers and articles, when are we going to talk about the fact that oppression replicates itself *within* the BME category as well?

Many do not realise that the idea of BME obscures the fact that racism can, and does, exist between people of colour. Anti-blackness, for instance, is present in many Arab and North African communities. The BME category suggests that white people are the only perpetrators of racism. It obscures the very sore, historical question of the role of Arabs, for example, in the slave trade. But where do you find spaces to have conversations about these issues when all the BME spaces at university are shared?

**Anti-blackness is inherent in a lot of [non-black BME people's] cultures, and I don't think they want to acknowledge that. – Fope**

**Why are we all forcing unity that's not there? – Kenya**

**When you pander to this whole solidarity thing, you make it seem like we're best friends and we're not. Living on a council estate, it's just loads of people of colour, and a lot of people**

**who are racist are also ethnic minorities.**
**– Courtney**

While I was at Cambridge, I was repeatedly asked by people I met if I went to the *other* university in Cambridge – because of course the notion that as a black woman, I might have earned a place at the best university in the country is difficult for some to conceive of. The first time I was ever asked this was by a boy of South Asian origin – even though I had just told him which Cambridge college I went to. His racialised assumptions about my academic abilities kicked in before his senses could, and he profiled me. Don't be deceived into thinking that the only racism that you're going to fight is going to come from white people. A lot of student political work and activism frames the conversation as white v. non-white – but be aware of what that lens obscures.

## #BlackMenofCambridgeUniversity and the Gendered Aspect

These conversations often gloss over the ways in which patriarchal dynamics penetrate these spaces, too. A lot of political work, especially that concerning anti-racism movements, relies on the hard work of women and queer people, which often goes ignored. This isn't a phenomenon unique to student activism, or even to this period in modern history. However, our viral #BlackMenofCambridgeUniversity campaign was another reminder of what that looks like.

On 25 April 2017, a friend of mine, Hepsi Adeosun, WhatsApped me a screenshot of a tweet that had gone viral. It was a group of black boys from Yale University with the hashtag #BlackMenofYaleUniversity, and the text read 'Omg make this happen pls, for Cam haha'. I laughed it off, and said I would run it by the ACS committee. Before I knew it, the committee was loving the idea, Hepsi was brainstorming a list of boys who might be willing, and I was charging my camera because we had to jump on a trending wave that could end up being a very powerful access initiative for Cambridge.

In the end, we managed to get fourteen black boys together for what would become one of my favourite memories of my time at Cambridge. It was a warm afternoon on 1 May. I set up a little tripod on the lawns of St John's College, in front of a neo-gothic archway, hoping to capture a poignant juxtaposition between the old, quintessential Cambridge from which people like us had been excluded for so long, and its growing cohort of black students that were defining the new age. The boys all knew each other, even if vaguely. But in this moment, it felt different. This didn't feel like a random group of lads. There was a genuine camaraderie, fraternity and infectious joy that I was really keen to capture. It felt magical just being there.

I had a revision presentation right after the shoot, and so I had to rush off. I took my laptop out once I arrived, but I sat at the back, editing photos for about twenty minutes. After another ten minutes, I had to walk out – I was too excited to stay. I ran home, where Chelsea was waiting for me, ready to compose this make-or-break Facebook caption, decide on the hashtags, and prepare all our social media platforms. We knew there was no turning back after we hit that 'Post' button. We had to make sure that not a single word could be misinterpreted, twisted by any mischievous people or picked up by the *Daily Mail* in attempts to slander the ACS or Cambridge's black community more broadly. Chelsea thought we needed numbers in the caption to stress why these initiatives were so important, so we looked up the admissions statistics and found out that in the year that we joined the university, only fifteen black boys had matriculated alongside us. I find it quite telling that we weren't even shocked by the discovery.

Our carefully crafted caption, posted on the ACS Facebook page, read:

**In 2015, only 15 black, male undergraduates were accepted into Cambridge.**

**However, it is important that despite their under-representation, we let young black people know that this is something that they can aspire to.**

**'Young black men don't grow up thinking they'll make it here. They should.' – Dami Adebayo (Robinson College)**

**Inspired by the viral image of young black men from Yale, the Cambridge ACS decided to capture just some of the black men who contribute to one of the world's most innovative intellectual spaces.**

**Representation matters.**

**#BlackBoyJoy**

**#BlackMenofCambridgeUniversity**

I don't exaggerate when I say 'carefully crafted'. We read it over again and again – and it paid off. We had about a thousand Facebook reactions within a few hours; we knew that this was going to be pretty big.

We posted the photos on the evening of 1 May. We wanted the campaign to go viral, so a media furore was welcomed. The morning after the pictures went out, I received a Twitter message from Victoria Sanusi, then at Buzzfeed. Thanks to her, Buzzfeed was the first publication to run a story on the photos on 2 May. As a black woman who has always used her voice to promote other black voices, we could trust that Victoria would do justice to the story.

**One of the first people to write about me was Victoria Sanusi, and just seeing a black woman writing about me in such a great way on such a huge platform such as Buzzfeed . . . that to me was sisterhood. – Courtney**

I remember being in a meeting and my phone kept ringing. I left the meeting, and listened to a string of voicemails from different newspaper outlets, asking for permission to use the pictures. Channel 4 followed Buzzfeed with a feature video for their online platform. Over the next few days, the pictures were broadcast on the BBC (online, World News and Victoria Derbyshire), the *Washington Post*, the *Evening Standard*, *Elle*, the *Mirror* and *The FADER*, to name just a few, and I and the boys featured did a variety of TV and radio interviews as well.

As the reach expanded, inevitably the criticisms got back to us. Numerous people were unhappy with the fact that there were no girls in the picture. We had a few explanations: firstly, we were just jumping on Yale's wave, but secondly, there were, and still are, unique issues that black boys face concerning representation, especially in the media. The news and mainstream media are much more likely to criminalise black boys than to show them thriving at an institution such as Cambridge. We weren't going to apologise for not focusing on black girls, who outnumbered black boys at Cambridge by over 50 per cent at the time. In 2015, the year of those fifteen black boys' admission, twenty-three black girls entered Cambridge. By 2017, in my final year, the figures stood at twenty-five black boys and thirty-three black girls. The underrepresentation of black students at Cambridge is poor – but it is worse still for black men, and we chose to focus on that.

Some people, however, weren't buying our explanations – and not because what we said wasn't true, but because for some, this campaign pointed to a broader underlying issue. Black women are used to doing the bulk of political work, while black men are the faces of the movements; black women are constantly taking it upon themselves to uplift black men, and address issues that affected them, with no reward or credit for them in return. The dynamic between who does the work and who gets credit for it falls along gendered lines.

This isn't a new phenomenon. 'Blacktivism', or race-related political work, has been riddled with this imbalance throughout history. When you think of 'Black Lives Matter', you're more likely to know who DeRay Mckesson is than the three women – Alicia Garza, Opal Tometi and Patrisse Cullors – who actually started the movement. Think further back to America's civil rights movements, and you think Martin Luther King Jr. – not the women who played key organisational roles in the movement. When you think of the Million Man March of 1995, you're more inclined to remember the prominent roles of the male speakers such as Jesse Jackson, and again, not the roles of women. The work of women such as Olive Morris, Funmilayo Ransome-Kuti and Claudia Jones is not lost on me. Women's labour is constantly being erased, while you don't have to look far to see how the legacies of men are memorialised.

In late September 2018, Cambridge held a month-long exhibition during Black History Month which featured portraits of ten notable black students and alumni. One of the boys I asked to feature in the Black Men of

Cambridge photos was included in the exhibition, simply because he had posed for my photos. But neither I, nor any other member of that Cambridge ACS committee who had organised the initiative, were honoured in the same way. Our ACS committee that year had eleven people on it, and ten of us were women, all of whom were elected. The only male member of the committee was not elected – we invited him to take up that role. Although the 2018–19 committee has more male committee members than I have ever seen in Cambridge ACS, and even a male president, the current president is the first male president that the society has had in ten years.

It's important to acknowledge that as black women in these spaces, we often outnumber black men. Aspiring for 50:50 representation in our activist work is hardly feasible. If there were more of us black women there, I shouldn't think that expecting us to use our platform to also lift up black men would be unreasonable. However, as black women, we spend a lot of time carrying the weight of everyone else, while finding our efforts ignored and unacknowledged.

For black queer people, this issue runs even deeper. Every single black queer person that I knew in Cambridge was engaged in political work. For the most part, they were the ones organising the protests, running the discussion groups and writing the open letters. I could never discuss the lack of representation in political work without honouring the black queer people who gave so much to fight for our black community in spite of the homophobia, transphobia and biphobia that they had to face.

**The women of colour and queer people of colour and non-binary people of colour – those are the people I know who are consistently doing work and who never get shouted out for it. – Arenike**

We are within our rights to question whether black, straight men in activist spaces are actively taking measures to resolve the erasure of black female voices. We must not forget that black men are still men, complicit in a patriarchal system that profits from the undervaluing of our labour. Some black men who share these spaces with us have not helped us when we're organising on the frontline, and have also not spoken up for us when our voices are silenced. Black men have male privilege in these spaces – but are they using that privilege to elevate the voices of the black women around them? Are the black men who can more easily adopt the 'cool' character in their groups of white friends speaking up for us? Are they challenging the misogynoir on our behalf in the rooms where we aren't present to defend ourselves?

**It's easier for a crowd of black men to fade into the white school population in a way that black girls just simply couldn't. – Saredo**

In my third year, a black mixed-race man in my year made a video in which he performed a freestyle (rap). He called out people like me who have spoken out extensively about the access issues facing black students in, and applying to, Cambridge. According to him, we were insinuating that 'you can't enjoy your time here [at university] if your skin is brown'. He was apparently very troubled by the fact that we were informing the rest of the world about the trials that come with being black at Cambridge because, he said, 'I enjoy Cambridge and I don't want a twisted version of my life being made money off by the papers.' Of *course* he was doing just fine; as a black (mixed-race) man, he could comfortably be the 'cool black guy' in his group of white friends in a way that I would never be able to. He just didn't see why black women like us might find Cambridge so hard. In response, I wrote a blog post entitled 'We need your support, not your freestyles'. I was also disappointed that, in spite of all his chat, it wasn't clear how he'd used his own relative privilege in Cambridge's spaces to uplift and empower those around him who struggle, or to offer help to those fighting our corner. Perhaps he did plenty that I don't know about. Whatever. One thing seems clear to me. It was easy for him to rap about 'the black experience' but I wished he would have matched that energy when we were looking for volunteers for our ACS Mentoring Scheme.

The gendered aspect of political work at university may infuriate you as it did me. I wanted to forgive black men for letting us down because they face their own challenges. After all, that was something that we tried to acknowledge with the Black Men of Cambridge campaign. My existence in this white space is hard enough – I don't want to have to fight black men too. And I don't think in-fighting does much to help the cause. On the other hand, I have had to accept that a lot of black men *will* let us down. I have learnt that there is work that we can do without them, and I have taken their presence, where it does exist, as an added bonus. I do my best to educate black men on how much the burden of this labour affects us, but I have stopped waiting for this to inspire them to speak up. So girls: if you choose to engage in political work, be prepared to take on an unfair amount of it – and be aware that if you are waiting for black men to lift you up too, you might be waiting a long time.

### Hypervisibility and the Media

As a black girl in Cambridge, you can't really hide.

**Being a black student in an elite space is being hypervisible because you are there. – Mikai**

Whiteness as a category is powerful because of how it others non-white people. Whiteness is the normative position from which other races are defined, and being white therefore means that you can blend into the background in a way that black people can't. We are hypervisible and identifiable, and it's hard to avoid the media, especially if you are engaged in any form of activism.

With the Benin Bronze campaign, we tried very hard to avoid the press. The campaign came just after Oxford's 'Rhodes Must Fall' campaign had really taken off, and the media were practically waiting for a Cambridge sequel to erupt so that they could pursue this dramatic storyline of Oxbridge under attack from raging liberal snowflakes (as the media likes to characterise us). We had to be super careful about what we said to anyone. We released one statement, and decided that would be it – but of course, the press wasn't going to relent. The papers picked up a post from my personal blog (which I quickly deleted) in which I said how proud I was of the progress we had made as a student body, and there were articles about our proposal in the *Guardian* and *Daily Mail* within a few days. I stupidly thought it would be a good idea to read through the comment section under the *Guardian* article, which was filled with people telling me to go back to my country, to be grateful to Cambridge for even giving me a place, and calling us troublemakers and 'attention-seeking students'. After the incident of the college OGM, I thought I had developed a thicker skin, but it was still disheartening to see how many strangers were against us.

Another important reason why we chose to stay away from the media, apart from the fact that we needed to focus on our dialogue with the university, was that we wanted to retain control of the narrative. We knew how easy it was for student politics to be twisted in the mainstream media. This is a lesson that ended up being very helpful when the Black Men of Cambridge campaign came around.

The day after our post, I turned my phone off, because I really did have exams to revise for – but when I switched it on for a few minutes, I got a call from the BBC inviting me to be on *Victoria Derbyshire Live*, a huge morning show. I abandoned my revision for the day, did my makeup, put on a smart jacket and headed to the BBC Cambridge studios. While I was there, I ended up doing *BBC World News* as well. This, for me, was amazing, because it meant that my parents could watch from Nigeria. On my way to the interview, Chelsea prepared a research document with all our key facts and figures, and calmed me down in anticipation of my first-ever live TV interview. We were on a roll. The ACS was receiving heaps of messages from parents thanking us for being an inspiring image for their children, from teachers, from big sisters and big brothers, but also from people who had seen the pictures, and now felt emboldened to make a Cambridge application. This was exactly the effect that we hoped the pictures would have.

A few days later, I got a call from an executive producer at Al Jazeera. (I still wonder how all these people got my number.) Al Jazeera for me has always been a news organisation that I admire because it challenges dominant narratives of non-Western countries in ways that I think are admirable. The producer wanted to bring me on to Femi Oke's show, *The Stream*. Femi Oke is one of the first black women I ever saw on TV when I was growing up, and as a fellow Nigerian, I was flattered by the request. This seemed like a big opportunity. However, they wanted to run a thirty-minute feature, without me, pitting the Cambridge black boys against the boys from Yale in a discussion about how awful it was to be at an elite, white-dominated university, connecting their experiences with police brutality, microaggressions and everyday racism at university.

I instinctively turned it down; it was straying so far from the positive narrative that we had set out to pursue. How do we show people that Cambridge is a place where black people can thrive, and in the same breath tell them that it's awful? Al Jazeera wouldn't budge. Femi Oke called me personally, and I had to tell a lady that I had looked up to for effectively my whole life that I could not honour her request. Someone went behind my back and reached out to the boys personally – but luckily we were all on the same page; they knew that this was a bad idea too. As a budding broadcast journalist, it could have been one of the best opportunities of my life. But I had to refuse it in the pursuit of something bigger. We had a story to protect. We were intentional about the message that we wanted this campaign to represent and we stuck to it – even when it meant turning down significant coverage from a global news outlet.

Fortunately, most of the coverage of the Black Men of Cambridge campaign was positive. There were exceptions, though. In the days following the campaign, Camilla Turner, the *Telegraph*'s education editor, interviewed one of the boys we had photographed. The headline that ran with her story was 'Britain's top universities should not be "attacked" for admitting low numbers of ethnic minority students' – even though she knew that this was not the message of our campaign.

This would not be the last time that the *Telegraph* misrepresented the facts behind one of Cambridge's black-centred movements. Later in 2017, the Decolonise English working group at Cambridge sent its open letter to the English department, asking them to diversify their reading lists. Unfortunately, it fell into the hands of the press. On 25 October 2017, a photograph of Lola Olufemi, a black woman who was then the CUSU Women's Officer, was plastered on the cover of the *Telegraph*, with the headline on their print edition reading, 'Student forces Cambridge to drop white authors'. This was another Camilla Turner story. Lola was vilified for her role in the campaign. Although she was only one of over 100 people who had signed the open letter to the faculty, as a black woman who had been at the frontline of the campaign she was a visible, easy target.

Her efforts to diversify the curriculum were about more than just 'seeking to exclude white men' from the syllabus. Reducing the movement to this was a clear misrepresentation, which sought to frame Lola as a troublemaker who didn't appreciate the contributions of white men to English.

**[The *Telegraph* was] misconstruing our claims for a more inclusive curriculum to be one of replacement or a kind of iconoclasm, which is**

**bullshit. I mean, I'm all for iconoclasm. We can literally shut Shakespeare off the curriculum – but that's not what the open letter said! – Arenike**

By placing Lola in particular on the cover, the *Telegraph* opened her up to abuse from racist trolls online. The next day, following over forty complaints to the press regulator IPSO, it issued a fickle correction, a discreet square inside the paper:

**The academics' proposals were in fact recommendations. Neither they nor the open letter called for the University to replace white authors with black ones and there are no plans to do so. We apologise to all concerned.**

But the damage had already been done. The *Telegraph* had succeeded in making Lola a scapegoat.

Many black students on the frontline have had similar experiences. Incidents like this force black activists to recede. Their rallying cries are reduced to whimpers by the fear of becoming the next target. As a black woman fighting to decolonise the curriculum, Lola represented both those who would benefit most from a diversified curriculum and those who had the most to lose from the fight.

**For many black people and [people of colour], you can't just put yourself in the limelight. If you're black, you're very identifiable. I'm not gonna go and occupy anything! – Arenike**

Media attention may expose you to other silencing mechanisms, too. When Stormzy announced his Cambridge scholarship programme, Chelsea was interviewed on Sky News, and mysteriously received an email from the university's communications team with 'tips' on how to discuss Cambridge in the interview.

**I just messaged him back: 'Hi. Thanks for these but I'm fine. Cheers. Chelsea.' He was basically telling me in a very coded way to be careful of what I say about Cambridge. – Chelsea**

When Mikai was featured on the BBC in a discussion about mental health at university, Warwick sent its university press officer to wait behind the scenes. '**I will say what I like, thank you very much!**' was her response to the university's attempt to stifle her. Universities are always working to make themselves look good. They even take credit for student labour that they've done next to nothing to meaningfully support, in order to make themselves look better. Regardless of their efforts to maintain their reputation, institutions have to be held accountable, and sometimes using the pressure of the media to speak up against them is the most power-ful tool you have to force a response. We're already being silenced by the press – but a university silencing you too? You have a right to speak out against your institution, and you should do so if you ever feel the need to – and you're brave enough.

I completely understand why black students choose to steer clear of media attention when they can, or even disengage from political work altogether. However, the media can also be used positively, and has played an important role in promoting black voices. While we were at Cambridge, Courtney and Renée made a video for Courtney's YouTube channel about their journey getting into Cambridge. Courtney was maligned by racists in the comments, and told that she was only accepted into the university to fulfil its diversity quota. When Courtney fought back, her comments went viral, she was able to use her interviews with media outlets such as Channel 4 and *Cosmopolitan* as a medium to continue to inspire black girls with her story.

Using the media in your political work can be fun sometimes – but be cautious or you'll risk becoming the media's black token. The Black Men of Cambridge campaign opened doors to many opportunities for me, particularly speaking ones. I had to try and make informed decisions about whether or not I was quali-fied to take up these opportunities, or whether I was being used by organisations hoping to tick their 'diversity' checklist. It became harder to tell whether *I* was using the media to get my message out there or the media was using me. I found myself winging a panel on 'Encountering Brexit', by the modern languages department, and was asked to do an interview on a BME orchestra coming to perform at a Cambridge music festival. Besides playing a few instruments when I was younger, nothing I had done indicated that I would be the most qualified person to speak on the importance of the orchestra's presence. It felt as if I was asked only because I was black and they had my phone number.

So, black girls, the chances of you finding yourself dealing with the press are higher than your white counterparts. It's the price of hypervisibility that no one prepared me for. It's up to you, but be aware of the potential risks before you make the call.

## Allyship, Oppression and
## Privilege in Activist Spaces

Some people grow disenchanted with student activism due to the way oppression and privilege may be replicated in these spaces. Whiteness and white privilege permeate all aspects of our society, and activist spaces, even anti-racism ones, are no exception. There are some white people who think they can explain racism better than the people who are victims of it, and who speak over BME people in the process. It's not always conscious: sometimes, the mere presence of white people in these spaces can see BME people code-switch, and even stay silent out of concern for white people's feelings. The white privilege may manifest in very subtle ways, or it may show itself more overtly. Either way, white privilege is pervasive, and working actively to decentre whiteness in activism is an ongoing battle.

**So much of these spaces are co-opted by white people. – Arenike**

Feminist societies can be quite a good example of this. Most of the feminist society events that I went to at Jesus College did a good job of ensuring that the discussion was intersectional and aware of the extent to which other axes of identity (for example, race) might affect your experience of your gender and other systems of oppression. However, many black feminists have struggled when they have attempted to have painful, radical and necessary discussions about white feminism and the extent to which race is so often excluded from these discussions. Fope was the president of the Feminist Society at Newcastle University. Their attempts to dismantle racism within feminist spaces got them into more trouble than they deserved:

> **I did workshops, like 'How to be an Ally' or like, 'Your Fave's a Racist'. I did one called 'The Suffragettes Were Racists, Sorry' – something like that. I did 'Jesus Wasn't White and Other White Lies' and stuff that clearly was meant to be provocative. And then I was reported to welfare [services] . . . I had a [Facebook] cover photo that said 'black pussy supremacy'. Someone reported me to welfare for that. – Fope**

Although there were no serious repercussions for their actions, Fope told me how much of a toll it took on their mental health. Someone, somewhere felt threatened by their attempts to decentre white people in these discussions, even in feminist spaces where black women and non-binary people should expect a degree of safety.

Try and convince your friends, especially the white and male friends, who may have relative privilege in these spaces to make efforts to decentre themselves, and to use their white privilege to uplift you, not silence you. They may call themselves allies, and while their presence can be helpful and is often necessary, being an ally isn't about hijacking our voices or taking over our spaces.

But it's also more than standing by and holding our hands.

**They don't understand that allyship is a doing word. You can't just call yourself an ally and like, that's the end of it. It's constantly unlearning problematic behaviours and a lot of them just don't have the time or range for it. – Fope**

Allyship requires you to have difficult conversations and call out racism in the communities we can't reach – in your own households, for example. It means educating people in your everyday life and finding ways to relieve our burden. It also requires understanding that sometimes we invite you into our spaces to listen, not to speak over us or for us.

Budding activists: white people may feel threatened by your radicalism. When you highlight their complicity in racist structures, they may close off (or cry), but if they're going to try and be allies to the cause and support you in your fight without themselves taking up space, then they have some work to do too.

## The A Word

Three years and a half-book later, I still don't know whether or not I would call myself an activist. I'm not alone in this internal battle. 'Activist' is an amorphous label that means something different to everyone. I've intentionally used the word quite loosely because I still don't know what it means. However, a common thread I have found is a sense of people feeling as if they have not done enough to earn the label. We hold activists to a higher moral standard. We expect them to always be ready to act. We expect them to always have the answers, and to be educated on the issues. Put that way, I see why some people may shy away from the term.

I would describe Fope as an activist, perhaps. Fope went to their first protest when they were in Year 10, and has worked tirelessly since secondary school creating spaces for women of colour, non-binary people of colour and queer people of colour, as well as educating people on the lack of diversity in white feminism. Yet they said to me, 'If I was going to write a bio, I don't know if I would say *activist*.'

There are also those who believe that to identify as an activist is to commit to a life of unyielding self-sacrifice for a larger cause.

**I think the position of an activist and the idea of it has been hugely diluted and hugely romanticised. True activism to me is laying down your life for a cause. – Courtney**

This is a standard so high that it's hard to imagine anyone realistically being able to measure up. There are also fears and risks attached to hypervisibility that not everyone is prepared to take on, and they disavow the label as a means of self-preservation. As a black activist, there is a lot at stake, and I hear that.

Despite the high standards to which we hold activists and the expectations we have of them, we must not undervalue contributions that may be less visible. Whether you're writing in resistance, or educating those around you, you have something to contribute to the movement.

**It's about the small steps that you're taking towards the big picture of change. – Ayomide**

The activist bar is always moving. You're going to come across people who think you haven't done enough groundwork, enough educating, or enough mobilising to be considered an activist. Whether or not you decide to call yourself an activist, *do activism*. It is so clichéd, but we literally own the future. University offers us a unique opportunity to be surrounded by equally passionate people, and the potential that students have as a group is both underestimated and extremely powerful. In whatever way you can, get involved and get on board.

We've got a system to fix.

## Epilogue

University was a steep but rewarding learning curve for both of us, filled with opportunities that we could never have dreamt of elsewhere. Most of all, it was a new challenge in many ways. We were pushed to limits we didn't know we had, academically and mentally, and we were strengthened in the process. We were forced to find our voices in spaces in which people like us had often been silenced. But most importantly, university put us in a position to take these new lessons and inspire people, especially black girls, who would come after us.

We must think about how racist and gendered stereotypes are imposed on us before we even make our university applications, inevitably capping our aspirations. From the national curriculum that ignores or misrepresents our stories to university reading lists that don't go far enough to remedy this, everything is directly relevant to what 'inclusion' means for black girls at university. Minority underrepresentation, and being unable to always articulate how that affects us, is taking a toll on our mental wellbeing, quality of life and ultimately, what we can get out of our time at university. We are forced to carve out our own spaces for our own benefit and protection.

We want to show everyone that when we talk about diversity and inclusion at university, we're not just pointing to abstract concepts, targets, theories and ideas. We are real people and these very conversations have a direct impact on our lives and university experiences. For once, we as students have decided to grab hold of this narrative and centre our voices in a conversation that only works if it is nuanced and critical. Black students across the country have been working tirelessly to address matters of diversity and inclusion for so long. We are not the first and we definitely will not be the last. We only hope that *Taking Up Space* will colour the existing conversation with the subjectivities of black students across the country. This is what it *feels* like to be a black girl at university. These trying years have birthed our inner fighters, equipped us with critical ideas, networks and support systems for facing the outside world.

To round off our interviews with our contributors, we asked, 'Was university worth it?'

**Well, a Cambridge degree, I'm hoping so! – Kenya**

**I absolutely do think it's worth it. It has inherent value, I believe, learning things and knowing things and just having options in your life. – Saredo**

**If you want to go 'big time corporate', yes. If you want to be a creative of any kind, it depends. – Mikai**

**No. Unless there's something you really, really want to study. I wouldn't say that I've ever been particularly challenged. And a lot of people I've talked to who didn't go to university and have apprenticeships, bitches got houses! – Fope**

**It's so worth it. It's expensive, but it's worth it. – Ayomide**

**I really think it is worth it if you do a degree that you care about. – Eireann**

**With all the pain, with all the sorrow, and all the joy mixed in, it was definitely worth it. – Renée**

If you asked us, we'd say that of course university was worth it. Academically, it is simultaneously the most independence we have ever had and the hardest we have ever been pushed. The geeks deep inside us still miss being surrounded by library books and journal articles on a daily basis, and learning to develop and articulate our ideas in new, deeper ways. Like us, you may find that the friendships that survive some of your most horrible experiences at university become some of the most valuable.

Our memories of university are ultimately not consumed with our worst confrontations with racist ignorance and isolation, which we have tried to suppress for our own self-preservation. When we look back, the memories we treasure most are the nights we spent laughing and crying over jollof, dancing our asses off at house parties, and being there to celebrate with each other and all our friends on the days that we graduated. University was worth it for us because it helped us learn more about ourselves; it was an exploration of our identities in ways we couldn't have expected. For Ọrẹ, it was an encounter with the visibility of her blackness in a way that her life in Nigeria, and an extremely diverse boarding school, had shielded her from. For Chelsea, it was defying a false, reductive stereotype about what it means to be a working-class black woman at university.

Above all, at university we realised that the concept of space means a lot more to us as black women. We have never been afforded the luxury of simply existing and being able to blend into the background. We are constantly forced to navigate university spaces that claim to support us but rarely show positive action proving that. So what do we do?

We organise in, and most importantly, create spaces. They become centres of validation, sisterhood, and the epicentre of radical critique. For us, university shouldn't be about claiming authority over the intellectual and the academic. Instead, it should become a place where we can disrupt the ideas of knowledge and knowledge production.

Leaving university has only gone to show that many of the issues we faced as black girls at university are replicated, and often intensified, in the world beyond it. Imposter syndrome may become easier to handle, but is unlikely to disappear. The thinly-veiled racist incidents will not become less common in the life that you pursue afterwards, and unfortunately, no less common either will be the people who do not consider your voice valid. We only hope that you take all that we, and our interviewees, have shared with you to go into this world fearlessly, lighting it up and taking up all the space you truly deserve.

# Notes

To access the links below online, please visit the *Taking Up Space* page on the Penguin UK website (www.penguin.co.uk/takingupspace).

## Introduction

8 'whitest universities in the country . . .'
https://www.undergraduate.study.cam.ac.uk/files/
publications/ug_admissions_statistics_2017_cycle_2.pdf
Published May 2018.

## Getting In

22 'In 2017-18, UK domiciled . . .'
https://www.advance-he.ac.uk/resources/2018_HE-stats-
report-students.pdf
Published in 2018.

22 'But as Professor of Race and Gender Heidi Mirza states . . .'
*Heidi Safia Mirza, Race, Gender and Educational Desire:*
*Why Black Women Succeed and Fail*
Published 2009.

26 'But with black Caribbean students three times . . .' https://
www.bbc.co.uk/news/education-44886153 Published in July
2018.

28 'Recruit more students from exclusively . . .' https://www.
suttontrust.com/newsarchive/oxbridge-over-recruits-from-
eight-schools/
Published in December 2018.

28 'Around 7 per cent of all UK school pupils attend' https://
guidetoindependentschools.com/key-independent-school-
statistics/

30 'What it's like being black and working class at Cambridge'
http://www.bbc.co.uk/newsbeat/article/41696224/what-
its-like-being-black-and-working-class-at-cambridge
Published October 2017.

31 ' . . . university student in the UK receives around' https://
thetab.com/uk/2019/02/28/mum-can-you-send-me-100-the-
universities-where-students-get-the-most-money-from-
their-parents-94157
Published February 2019.

33 'Reni Eddo-Lodge sums this up perfectly . . .'
Reni Eddo-Lodge, *Why I'm No Longer Talking to White*
*People About Race*, p. 207.
Published June 2017.

34 'The Sutton Trust found that some groups . . .'
https://www.suttontrust.com/wp-content/uploads/2016/11/
Class-differences-report_References-available-online.pdf
Published November 2016.

35 'For example, in Northern Ireland, black ethnic groups . . .'
https://www.bbc.co.uk/news/education-44226434
Published May 2018.

37 'The three universities with the biggest black student . . .'
https://www.bbc.co.uk/news/education-44226434
Published May 2018 (as above).

37 'After students from Bangladeshi backgrounds . . .'
https://www.bath.ac.uk/publications/diverse-places-of-
learning-home-neighbourhood-ethnic-diversity-ethnic-
composition-of-universities/attachments/diverse-places-
of-learning.pdf
Published August 2017.

38 'Social Market Foundation found that more than one in
ten'
https://www.independent.co.uk/news/uk/home-news/
black-students-drop-out-university-figures-a7847731.html
Published July 2017.

38 'This has led someone to claim a form of 'self-segregation . . .'
https://www.bbc.co.uk/news/education-40926117
Published August 2017.

39 'Coventry University, for example, is 54.5 per cent white
and 44.5 per cent BME. From the outset, there's strength in
numbers . . .'
https://www.coventry.ac.uk/globalassets/media/documents/
equality-and-diversity/statistics-2017-18/eandd-web-
statistics-all-students-31012018.pdf
Published January 2018.

40 'Professor David Gilborn, Director of the Centre . . .'
https://www.tes.com/news/tes-talks-todavid-gillborn
Published January 2017.

40 'Institutional racism can be defined as the collective . . .'
https://www.ucu.org.uk/media/9526/Investigating-
higher-education-institutions-and-their-views-on-the-
Race-Equality-Charter/pdf/Race_Equality_Charter_
Kalwant_Bhopal_Clare_Pitkin.pdf
Published September 2018.

40 'In 2018, the independent reported on data which revealed . . .'

https://www.independent.co.uk/news/education/
education-news/black-students-university-uk-racism-
ucas-application-a8376501.html
Published May 2018.

41 'Black and minority ethnic students of all backgrounds . . .'
https://www.bbc.co.uk/news/education-44226434
Published May 2018 (as above).

43 'Strategic objectives from the University of York's Equality . . .'
https://www.york.ac.uk/admin/eo/EDIStrategy/EDandI-
Strategy-Nov2017.pdf
Published November 2017.

44 'If you think I'm being harsh, have a look at SOAS . . .'
https://www.soas.ac.uk/equality-diversity-and-inclusion-
strategy/file113520.pdf
Published July 2016.

45 'A report by Professor Kalwant Bhopal and Clare Pitkin . . .'
https://www.ucu.org.uk/media/9526/Investigating-
higher-education-institutions-and-their-views-on-the-
Race-Equality-Charter/pdf/Race_Equality_Charter_
Kalwant_Bhopal_Clare_Pitkin.pdf
Published September 2018.

45 'In 2016, 1.5 per cent of the Cambridge . . .'
https://www.bbc.co.uk/news/education-44226434
Published May 2018 (as above).

46 'The letter stated that Cambridge . . .'
https://www.cam.ac.uk/news/open-letter-on-diversity-
in-admissions
Published June 2018.

47 'At Pembroke College, a BME . . .'
https://www.varsity.co.uk/news/14897
Published February 2018.

48 'Oxford ACS's Annual Access Conference . . .'
https://annualaccessconference.co.uk/

48 'Oxford have increased by 24.1 per cent . . .'

https://www.huffingtonpost.co.uk/renee-kapuku/being-
black-at-oxbridge-w_b_18368164.html?guccounter=1
Published September 2017.

49 'As Renée writes for the Huffington Post . . .'
As above.

51 'Target Oxbridge's partnership with both universities . . .'
http://www.ox.ac.uk/news/2018-02-16-success-and-expansion-
target-oxbridge-programme-black-teenagers
Published February 2018.

## #AcademiaSoWhite

55 'The history curriculum, for example . . .'
https://www.gov.uk/government/publications/national-
curriculum-in-england-history-programmes-of-study
Published September 2013.

55 'Primary schools are only required . . .'
https://assets.publishing.service.gov.uk/government/
uploads/system/uploads/attachment_data/file/239035/
PRIMARY_national_curriculum_-_History.pdf
Published September 2013

60 'a black attainment gap at a university level that doesn't
correlate with how well black students perform at GCSE
stage . . .'
https://assets.publishing.service.gov.uk/government/
uploads/system/uploads/attachment_data/file/439867/
RR439B-Ethnic_minorities_and_attainment_the_
effects_of_poverty_annex.pdf.pdf
https://www.advance-he.ac.uk/resources/2018_HE-stats-
report-students.pdf
Published June 2015.

61 'Black students make up 8 percent . . .'
https://www.advance-he.ac.uk/resources/2018_HE-stats-
report-students.pdf

Published September 2018.

61 'Only 2.4 per cent of students [ . . .] for the creative arts . . .'
https://royalhistsoc.org/wp-content/uploads/2018/10/
RHS_race_report_EMBARGO_0001_18Oct.pdf
Published October 2018.

64 'Over 10 per cent of students . . .'
As above.

64 'According to research by the Resolution Foundation . . .'
https://www.bloomberg.com/diversity-inclusion/blog/
people-ethnic-minorities-still-facing-major-jobs-gap-uk/
Published October 2018.

68 'Cambridge's Varsity newspaper featured a . . .'
https://www.varsity.co.uk/features/16174
Published October 2018.

70 'he was largely responsible for the deaths . . .'
https://www.independent.co.uk/news/world/world-
history/winston-churchill-genocide-dictator-shashi-
tharoor-melbourne-writers-festival-a7936141.html
Published September 2017.

73 'Academics such as Lundy Braun . . .'
https://journalofethics.ama-assn.org/article/avoiding-
racial-essentialism-medical-science-curricula/2017-06
Published June 2017.

74 'Chanda Prescod-Weinstein expands on this in her . . .'
https://medium.com/@chanda/decolonising-science-
reading-list-339fb773d51f#.0m5w2ivfq
Published June 2015, last updated May 2017.

74 'Akala spoke about it at the Oxford Union . . .'
https://www.youtube.com/watch?v=WUtAxUQjwB4
Published 26 November 2015.

75 'It is generally far more difficult . . .'
https://liberatingthecurriculumblog.wordpress.
com/2017/09/17/personal-experiences/
Published September 2017.

75 'According to a 2018 NHS report, "four times more likely to be 'sectioned" . . .'
https://digital.nhs.uk/data-and-information/publications/statistical/mental-health-act-statistics-annual-figures/2017-18-annual-figures
Published October 2018.

76 'That almost a third of UK graduate doctors . . .'
https://www.gmc-uk.org/static/documents/content/SoMEP-2017-final-executive-summary.pdf
Published December 2017.

88 'Data released by the Higher Educations Statistics Agency . . .'
https://www.hesa.ac.uk/news/19-01-2017/sfr243-staff
Published January 2017.

89 'A shockingly small 1.8 per cent . . .'
https://www.advance-he.ac.uk/resources/2018_HE-stats-report-staff.pdf
Published October 2018.

89 'Asian staff . . .'
As above.

89 'Considering just black women . . .'
As above and https://www.theguardian.com/education/2018/sep/07/uk-university-professors-black-minority-ethnic
Published September 2018.

92 'We welcomed the announcement in 2017 . . .'
https://www.theguardian.com/education/2017/may/28/oxford-students-to-get-exam-on-non-white-non-european-history
Published May 2017.

94 'ranked second in the country for sociology"''
The *Guardian* University Guide 2019: League Table for Sociology: https://www.theguardian.com/education/ng-interactive/2018/may/29/university-guide-2019-league-table-for-sociology

94 'in an online 'global social theory' reading list . . .'

https://globalsocialtheory.org/resources/reading-lists/

96 'In the same paper at Warwick . . .'
See 'Epic into Novel' paper. https://warwick.ac.uk/fac/arts/
english/undergraduate/uow_english_ug_prospectus_
online.pdf

98 'all but one of the countries tried by the International
Criminal Court . . .'
https://www.icc-cpi.int/pages/situations.aspx

101 'Chanda Prescod-Weinstein writes . . .'
https://medium.com/@chanda/making-meaning-of-
decolonising-35f1b5162509
Published February 2017.

103 'According to a 2018 report by Advance HE . . .'
https://www.advance-he.ac.uk/sites/default/files/2018_
HE-stats-report-students.pdf
Published October 2018.

## Mental Health

109 'In 2015–16, over 15,000 first-year students (UK-based)
disclosed mental health issues . . .'
https://www.bbc.co.uk/news/education-41148704
Published September 2017.

109 'Yet a Freedom of Information request by the Liberal
Democrat . . .'
https://www.independent.co.uk/news/uk/politics/students-
mental-health-support-waiting-times-counselling-
university-care-diagnosis-treatment-liberal-a8124111.html
Published January 2018.

109 'At the University of Bristol alone, there were ten suicides . . .'
https://www.theguardian.com/uk-news/2018/may/10/
university-of-bristol-confirms-sudden-death-of-first-
year-student
Published May 2018.

110 'The University of Cumbria, for example . . .'
https://www.ippr.org/files/2017-09/1504645674_not-by-degrees-170905.pdf
Published September 2017.

113-4 'Black British and non-British women were both found to be more . . .'
https://www.mentalhealth.org.uk/statistics/mental-health-statistics-black-asian-and-minority-ethnic-groups
Published 2014.

113-4 'The *Guardian* began its Racial Bias series . . .'
https://www.theguardian.com/uk-news/2018/dec/03/from-football-to-dating-to-tv-10-areas-rife-with-racial-bias-in-uk
Published December 2018.

114 'From the words 'MONKEY' and 'NIGGA' found written on Warwick student Faramade Ifaturoti's bunch of bananas . . .'
https://www.theguardian.com/education/2016/apr/08/bananagate-highlights-racism-among-warwick-students
Published April 2016.

114 'to fellow students chanting 'we hate the blacks' outside Rufaro Chisango's room at Nottingham Trent University . . .'
https://www.theguardian.com/commentisfree/2018/mar/11/racist-universities-not-tolerant-rugaro-chisango-nottingham-trent
Published March 2018.

117 'At Bath Spa University, a photo exhibition . . .'
https://www.bathspasu.co.uk/opps/blackhistorymonth/blackexcellenceblog/

123 'For starters, black men and women are more likely to engage . . .'
https://www.mentalhealth.org.uk/a-to-z/b/black-asian-and-minority-ethnic-bame-communities

126 'came up more than once in students' testimonials . . .'

https://www.theguardian.com/commentisfree/2018/
may/21/identity-matters-black-students-black-
therapists-cambridge-university
Published May 2018.

127 'Similarly, the Black, African and Asian Therapy Network
(BAATN)...'
https://www.baatn.org.uk/

128 'A study completed by Student Minds found that...'
https://www.studentminds.org.uk/uploads/3/7/8/4/
3784584/180129_student_mental_health__the_role_
and_experience_of_academics__student_minds_pdf.
pdf
Published January 2018.

## Finding Spaces

145 'Pauline Clance and Suzanne Imes, the psychologists...'
https://psycnet.apa.org/record/1979-26502-001
Published 1978.

148 'A whopping 79 per cent of respondents to a...'
https://www.nus.org.uk/en/news/press-releases/new-survey-
shows-trends-in-student-drinking/
Published September 2018.

148 'Young adults are the most likely...'
https://www.ons.gov.uk/peoplepopulationandcommunity/
healthandsocialcare/drugusealcoholandsmoking/bulletins/
opinionsandlifestylesurveyadultdrinkinghabitsingreat
britain/2017
Published May 2018.

150 'In 2017, a group of black students...'
https://thetab.com/uk/cardiff/2017/04/28/they-said-
they-didnt-want-an-urban-feel-cardiff-students-tell-us-
their-experiences-of-racism-in-nightclubs-27092
Published 2017.

152  'The NUS in 2018 . . .'
https://www.nus.org.uk/en/news/press-releases/
new-survey-shows-trends-in-student-drinking/
Published September 2018.

158  'FLY, which I learned stands for . . .'
https://flygirlsofcambridge.com/

159  'Warwick's Anti-Racism Society . . .'
https://www.facebook.com/groups/warsoc.2015.2016/?fref=ts

164-5  'The university's most recent admissions . . .'
https://www.undergraduate.study.cam.ac.uk/sites/www.
undergraduate.study.cam.ac.uk/files/publications/ug_
admissions_statistics_2017_cycle_4.pdf
Published May 2018.

## Desirability and Relationships

176  'The One Day University Love Survey stated that the top
five universities . . .'
https://tsrmatters.com/blog/one-fifth-of-british-students-
meet-the-love-of-their-life-on-campus/

177  'To be honest, there isn't really much of a dating scene . . .'
https://blackballad.co.uk/views-voices/navigating-the-
dating-scene-as-a-socially-conscious-black-woman?listId
s=590867cea8c0bab2039c3ac5
Published February 2019.

177  'Caren M. Holmes's essay . . .'
https://openworks.wooster.edu/cgi/viewcontent.
cgi?referer=https://www.google.com/&httpsredir=1&artic
le=1026&context=blackandgold
Published 2018.

194  'Stonewall's LGBT in Britain's Universities Report . . .'
https://www.stonewall.org.uk/system/files/lgbt_in_
britain_universities_report.pdf
Published 2018.

194 'The University of Oxford's Trans . . .'
https://www.oxfordsu.org/resources/lgbtq/TRANS-
REPORT-2018/
Published November 2018.

197 'Think Jamie and Nikki . . .'
https://www.youtube.com/watch?v=46xhFCXBMJs
Published May 2013.

197 'or HelloBianca, a channel amassing 55,000 subscribers . . .'
https://www.youtube.com/watch?v=nmc9Fakbx1Q&t=1s
Published January 2018.

200 'As such, many black queer men . . '
https://metro.co.uk/2019/03/22/as-a-black-gay-man-i-am-
constantly-reduced-to-outdated-racist-stereotypes-when-
online-dating-8889330/
Published March 2019.

202 'in an article titled "I'm not an object or a toy for your
white gaze" . . .'
https://metro.co.uk/2018/09/18/im-not-an-object-or-a-toy-
for-your-white-gaze-dont-fetishise-me-as-a-black-man-
7957474/
Published September 2018.

205 'A survey conducted by Hexjam looked at the sex lives . . .'
https://www.bustle.com/articles/91951-7-things-to-know-
about-students-sex-lives-in-the-uk-according-to-a-new-
survey
Published June 2015.

206 'The session included a video called "Tea and Consent" . . .'
https://www.youtube.com/watch?v=oQbei5JGiT8
Published May 2015.

206 'The body is an appropriate cultural symbol . . .'
https://journals.sagepub.com/doi/full/10.1177/
2374623816680622
Published December 2016.

207 'In my second year at university, I will never forget . . .'

*Danielle L. McGuire, "It Was Like All of Us Had Been Raped": Sexual Violence, Community Mobilisation, and the African American Freedom Struggle", JAH (2004), pp.910–920.*
Published 2004.

207 'Burke told ESSENCE magazine . . .'
https://www.essence.com/videos/tarana-burke-explains-why-black-women-dont-think-metoo-is-for-them/
Published November 2018.

208 '62 per cent of students and graduates have experienced sexual violence . . .'
https://revoltsexualassault.com/research/
Published March 2018.

208 'Only 2 per cent of those . . .'
As above.

208 '33 per cent have no knowledge or very little knowledge'
As above.

209 'The NUS project "That's What She Said" found . . .'
https://www.nus.org.uk/Global/Campaigns/That's%20what%20she%20said%20full%20report%20Final%20web.pdf
Published 2013.

210 'Comments included, "Sometimes it's fun to just go wild and rape 100 girls" . . .'
https://theboar.org/2018/05/warwick-students-temporarily-suspended/
Published May 2018.

210 'First of all, the university's director of press was appointed . . .'
https://www.bbc.co.uk/news/uk-47090864?SThisFB&fbclid=IwAR1Gyg-lbX_MbeUvxxwmgLJ_vrQ5GF3bbafNhP8DhGzTaIoHeoXOdTe-Qxs
Published February 2019.

211 'In 1994, the Zellick Report was published . . .'
https://universityapp..co.uk/sites/default/files/field/
attachment/NUS%20Zellick%20report%20briefing.pdf
Published 2015.

213 'Manchester Student Union have rallied around the night . . .'
https://manchesterstudentsunion.com/reclaimthenight

**'Blacktivism'**

232 'Some say it developed . . .'
https://www.bbc.com/news/uk-politics-43831279
Published May 2018.

238 'Our carefully crafted caption . . .'
https://www.facebook.com/cambridge.acs/posts/
in-2015-only-15-black-male-undergraduates-were-
accepted-into-cambridge-however-i/1881865065434347/
Published May 2017.

239 'Over the next few days . . .'
https://www.bbc.com/news/uk-39787690
https://www.washingtonpost.com/news/worldviews/
wp/2017/05/03/cambridge-has-a-problem-with-diversity-
these-black-men-just-illustrated-it-perfectly/?noredirect=
on&utm_term=.23e09f8b5aa9
https://www.standard.co.uk/lifestyle/london-life/why-a-
photo-of-14-young-black-cambridge-students-has-gone-
viral-a3529081.html
https://www.mirror.co.uk/news/real-life-stories/photo-
14-young-black-men-10347398
https://www.elle.com/uk/life-and-culture/news/
a35540/14-black-male-cambridge-students-pose-for-
photo-important-message/
https://www.thefader.com/2017/05/04/black-men-
cambridge-acs

All Published May 2017.

240 'We weren't going to apologise . . .'
https://www.undergraduate.study.cam.ac.uk/sites/www.
undergraduate.study.cam.ac.uk/files/publications/
undergrad_admissions_statistics_2015_cycle.pdf
Published May 2016.

240 'By 2017, in my final year . . .'
https://www.undergraduate.study.cam.ac.uk/sites/www.
undergraduate.study.cam.ac.uk/files/publications/ug_
admissions_statistics_2017_cycle_4.pdf
Published May 2018.

241 'One of the boys I asked to feature . . .'
https://www.cam.ac.uk/BlackCantabs
Published September 2018.

242 'Although the 2018-19 . . .'
https://cambridgeacs.org/committee/
Last updated in 2018.

244 'In response, I wrote . . .'
https://flygirlsofcambridge.com/2018/01/21/we-need-
your-support-not-your-freestyles-ore-ogunbiyi/
Published January 2018.

246 'The papers picked up . . .
https://www.theguardian.com/education/2016/feb/21/
cambridge-colleges-bronze-cockerel-must-go-back-to-
nigeria-students-say
https://www.dailymail.co.uk/news/article-3457159/After-
Cecil-Rhodes-s-Alcock-rooster-Students-call-bronze-
cockerel-sent-Africa-new-Oxbridge-college-row.html
Both published February 2016.

249 'In the days following the campaign . . .'
https://www.telegraph.co.uk/news/2017/05/03/dont-blame-
cambridge-lack-black-students-saysleading-students/
Published May 2017.

250 'On 25 October 2017 . . .'

https://www.telegraph.co.uk/education/2017/10/24/
cambridge-decolonise-english-literature/
Published October 2017

251 'The next day, following . . .'
https://www.ipso.co.uk/rulings-and-resolution-
statements/ruling/?id=19341-17
https://www.thedrum.com/news/2017/10/29/telegraph-
story-which-claimed-cambridge-student-was-forcing-
faculty-drop-white
Both published October 2017.

253 'While we were at Cambridge . . .'
https://www.youtube.com/watch?v=ICmuDCpDARQ
Published October 2015.

# Our Favourite Reads

Ayobami Adebayo, *Stay With Me*

Tomi Adeyemi, *Children of Blood and Bone*

Chimamanda Adichie, *Purple Hibiscus*

Beverley Bryan, Stella Dadzie, and Suzanne Scafe, *Heart of the Race, Black Women's Lives in Britain*

Brittney Cooper, *Eloquent Rage: A Black Feminist Discovers Her Superpower*

Jacquelyn Dowd Hall, 'The Long History of the Civil Rights Movement'

Reni Eddo-Lodge, *Why I'm No Longer Talking to White People About Race*

Frantz Fanon, *Black Skin, White Masks*

Frantz Fanon, *The Wretched of the Earth*

Tanisha C. Ford, 'Soul Style on Campus', from *Liberated Threads: Black Women, Style, and the Global Politics of Soul* (2015).

Yaa Gyasi, *Homegoing*

Patricia Hill Collins, *Black Feminist Thought: Knowledge, Consciousness and the Politics of Empowerment*

Afua Hirsch, *Brit-ish*

bell hooks, 'Is Paris Burning?'

C. L. R. James, *The Black Jacobins*

Jennie Livingston, *Paris is Burning* (docufilm: 1990)

Danielle L. McGuire, 'It Was Like All of Us Had Been Raped': Sexual Violence, Community Mobilisation, and the African American Freedom Struggle'

Walter Rodney, *How Europe Underdeveloped Africa*

Taiye Selasi, *Ghana Must Go*

Lola Shoneyin, *The Secret Lives of the Four Wives* (previously *The Secret Lives of Baba Segi's Wives*)

Chika Unigwe, *On Black Sisters' Street*

Alice Walker, *The Color Purple*

# Resources

Royal Historical Society Race Report
https://royalhistsoc.org/racereport/

Global Social Theory Reading Lists
https://globalsocialtheory.org/resources/reading-lists/
(includes HSPS Alternative Reading List)

FLY Cambridge
https://flygirlsofcambridge.com/

Gal-Dem
http://gal-dem.com/

My Body Back Project
http://www.mybodybackproject.com/notes-of-love/

The Elms, Cambridge
https://www.theelmssarc.org/

The Samaritans
https://www.samaritans.org/

Reporting Hate Crime
https://www.met.police.uk/true-vision-report-hate-crime/

Epigeum
https://www.epigeum.com/courses/support-wellbeing/consent-matters-boundaries-respect-and-positive-intervention/

Women Against Rape
www.womenagainstrape.net

The Runnymede Trust
https://www.runnymedetrust.org/projects-and-publications/education.html

Confident and Killing It
http://www.confidentandkillingit.com/

Click Relationships
https://clickrelationships.org/the-mix/

NHS Advice on Sexual Health for Young People
https://www.nhs.uk/live-well/sexual-health/
15-things-young-people-should-know-about-sex/

1752 Group
https://1752group.com/

Higher Educational Statistical Report 2018
https://www.ecu.ac.uk/publications/equality-higher-
education-statistical-report-2018/

Imkaan
https://www.imkaan.org.uk/

# Acknowledgements

## Chelsea

Firstly, a huge thank you to Akua, Stormzy and the whole #Merky Team for making *Taking Up Space* possible. I will be forever grateful that you gave us this opportunity to tell such an important story and archive our history.

To our wonderful and amazing agent, Carrie, this whole book would never have taken off without you. Thank you for always fighting our corner, for your honesty and brilliant ideas.

To everyone at Penguin Random House, especially Tom, Kate, Alice and Natalia, for investing time, for your dedication and for matching Ọrẹ's and my energy every single time, right from the beginning. From edits to making sure everything surrounding us has stayed as authentic as possible. Most importantly, for understanding how urgent and important this conversation is. Thank you for letting us be US!

To Courtney, Arenike, Mikaï, Micha, Kenya, Saredo, Adaobi, Ayomide, Barbara, Saskia, Fope, Renée, Eireann and Nathania. THANK YOU. Thank you for sharing your stories, experiences and past traumas. You're all brilliant and it goes without saying that this book wouldn't be possible without you.

To the Kwakye Krew, Mum, Dad, Jeanette, Louie, Toks and my biggest cheerleader, Joe, thank you for keeping me grounded, critical and unapologetic.

Finally, to my right-hand, best-friend and sister, Oreoluwa. Our friendship has only strengthened throughout this whole process. We always said if we could survive Cambridge, we could do anything. Well . . . I'm sure this nearly pushed us to the edge. But, I wouldn't have it any other way! I love you.

## Ọrẹ

First up, I need to thank God. I'm so grateful and so blessed to have had the opportunity to write this book and to share our stories with the world. I thank God for His grace and loving guidance throughout this whole process.

To my family, thank you for being behind me every step of the way. Thank you dad for staying up with me night after night to help me edit my chapters. Thank you mum for always answering my daily FaceTime calls, even when you're really busy. To Brother Toks, Anu, Aunty Dami and Mo for helping me make all the big decisions I was too indecisive to make myself. To the whole Ogunbiyi clan and beyond, I love you all.

To my friends who have had to put up with me while I've been stressed with deadlines, thank you for being understanding when I missed your calls, when I didn't have time to come out with you or if I ever forgot to check up on you. Now we can make up for all the lost time, I promise.

To the interviewees, you guys made this book. The interviews that we had made me feel nostalgic, happy, sad and every emotion in between. Thank you for shar-ing your experiences with us and with the world. Thank you for always replying to our annoying emails (and even the follow-ups). We really appreciate you.

However, none of this would have even been possible without the #Merky Books and Penguin squads. Stormzy, thank you for recognising that our stories need to be told and we hope we've done you proud. Akua, thank you for helping us bring our dream to life. Thank you for always letting us know that you're there if we need you. Thank you Tom Avery for giving up so much of your time to make sure that this book turned out the best it could be. To Kate, Natalia, Alice and everyone on the Penguin side, thank you for all your efforts.

To our agent turned wingwoman, Carrie. We knew from the first day we spoke to you that we'd be hard-pressed to find anyone who believed in this book more than you. Thank you for helping us through this new and sometimes scary process and for always having our best interests at heart.

TO MY OTHER HALF AND BESTIE BAE CHELS. We did it. I can't believe it. Thank you for not getting sick of me. Thank you for keeping me going. Thank you for going to all the meetings that couldn't wait and replying to emails when the time difference was killing me. We smashed it. It's me and you against the world babygirl.

For more information about *Taking Up Space*, please follow:

Twitter: **@takingupspacebk**

Instagram: **@takingupspacebook**